TALK THE TALK

TALK THE TALK
SPEECH AND DEBATE MADE EASY

By Alim Merali

GRAVITAS
PUBLISHING

Edmonton, Alberta

12 11 10 09 08 07 06   1 2 3 4 5

Library and Archives Canada Cataloguing in Publication

Merali, Alim, 1984-
    Talk the talk : speech and debate made easy / by Alim Merali.

Includes bibliographical references and index.
ISBN 0-9738682-0-1

    1. Debates and debating. I. Title.

PN4181.A45 2006   808.53   C2005-904345-8

The arguments and evidence presented should not be taken as the true opinions or factually correct research, respectively, of the author or publisher of this book. They are included solely for purposes of illustration, not for purposes of advocacy or information. The topics and resolutions listed in this publication are intended as sample issues only and should not be viewed as opinion declarations by the aforesaid parties.

Printed and bound in Canada by Friesens.
Printed on acid-free paper.

Book design by Optamedia.

www.talkthetalk.ca

DISCLAIMER

Debate is a dangerous sport.

Neither the author nor the publisher assume any liability whatsoever for bruised egos, classroom eruptions, dinner-table debacles, street-corner spectacles, or chaotic committees that reading *Talk the Talk* may cause.

Avoid debating at parties, banquets, family get togethers, and other social functions. Some of the common side-effects include friends pretending to care when they don't and people around you slowly backing away. In severe cases, you may wind up as the only person in the debate.

If, after reading *Talk the Talk*, you become addicted to arguing, seek immediate medical attention.

Table of Contents

To those who have taught me the sport of debate.

Foreword

Discover the Art of Speech and Debate

TAKING TALK TO THE NEXT LEVEL

We're surrounded by speech and debate everyday and everywhere, so it's no surprise that we often view oral communication as a natural, effortless activity. But is everyone you hear equally clear or equally convincing? Or do some people stand out, capturing your attention and securing your agreement?

There's a big difference between talking effortlessly and communicating effectively. Talking takes little effort, requiring others only to hear what you have to say. Communicating is much more advanced. Your audience has to be motivated—motivated by you, that is—to listen, understand, and respond favorably.

Similarly, there's a big difference between stating your opinion and presenting an argument. Stating an opinion calls on you to say what's on your mind, essentially making conversation or going with your gut instinct. Presenting an argument calls for convincing logic, clear structure, and confident delivery. A strong argument compels others to agree with your perspective or to take the action you want.

THE STYLE OF SUCCESS

If you think that great speakers and debaters are dry, think again! They often use humor, and they keep their audiences engaged and interested in what they're saying. Most importantly, they enjoy what they do, which becomes apparent in the expressiveness of their delivery. They're interesting and dynamic people—or at least speech and debate brings out their 'concealed' personalities.

Great speakers and debaters have a variety of styles. Some are powerful communicators because of their convincing tone, commanding stage presence, and passionate oration. Others are just as successful by presenting thoughtful, intelligent ideas with a calm and methodical style. Excellent communication skills aren't exclusive to the most talkative among us.

Despite the diversity of styles, there are certain traits common to all effective speakers and debaters. They have a sound grasp of structure, making sure that their speeches flow well. Delivering clearly and confidently, they captivate their audiences. Most importantly, they have the right attitude. They want to improve their skills, and they enjoy new challenges. They're active listeners who strive to learn from what others have to say.

WHY BOTHER?

Debating is one of the oldest and most common art forms. From Aristotle to John F. Kennedy, dinner tables to national legislatures, and students to seniors, the art of debate has been used to discuss competing views for centuries.

Throughout 25 years as a speech arts teacher, I've seen students become confident communicators and talented debaters. Discovering the art of speech and debate isn't easy. It does take hard work and dedication. And what's the result? I've witnessed hundreds of young leaders unearth their vocal potential to achieve success in their schools, communities, and careers.

The case for achieving excellence in speech extends much further than competition. You'll gain a powerful life skill guaranteed to improve your performance every time you communicate. Effective speaking enhances your performance in school presentations and class discussions. It helps you take charge in leadership positions and makes you shine in interviews for jobs, awards, and scholarships. Less tangible, but equally important, is how it improves your confidence whenever you deal with people.

Learning to debate will help you become more logical when you examine issues, thoughtful when you come up with ideas and insights, and convincing when you argue your perspective. In addition, you'll become more confident talking about what you already know. What use are biology, chemistry, history, and literature if you aren't comfortable articulating your knowledge to others? In today's competitive world, it's not enough to know the right answer. It's just as important to know how to *communicate* your knowledge to others.

PRACTICE MAKES (ALMOST) PERFECT

Speech and debate can't be learned through reading alone. If you want to discover this art, enjoy *Talk the Talk* and put what you learn to good use in your everyday activities. I can't emphasize enough how important it is to make speech and debate part of your daily routine. Participate in class discussions, debate social and world issues at the dinner table, and get involved in practice rounds. Also, you should join a debate club and compete in tournaments. If one isn't already established at your school, get a few friends together and start one up. Competitions will give you an opportunity to put your skills to the test against other students. Your experiences may even take you across the country or around the world.

Enjoy learning speech and debate and developing your own dynamic style. Individuals who excel at this powerful and necessary skill will be a step ahead in achieving success.

Shirley Konrad
Founder and Director
The Speech Studio Inc.

de‣bate (di-'bAt)
vb.

1 : to compete for victory in the sport of the mind **2** : to engage an opponent in a spirited battle of ideas **3** : to advance a view through powerful arguments, high-impact clash, and dynamic style

ROAD MAP:
GEAR UP TO TALK THE TALK

Part I

Introduction

Why Debate is the Sport of the Mind

From hockey players driving toward the net to skiers gliding down a hill, athletes put their bodies to the test every time they compete. They do so in their thirst for victory. Some define victory as reaching their personal best, such as beating their scoring record from the year before or achieving their fastest ever racing time. Others see victory as rising above the competition and ascending to the top of the podium.

Can the same be said for debaters? At first, the comparison seems frivolous. Debate doesn't require physical prowess. A debater can't get injured in the heat of competition (at least we hope not!). And a debater doesn't put his or her body through a grueling physical test.

The sport of debate exists in the *mind*. It requires mental prowess, as opposed to physical prowess. Any injury is to one's intellectual pride and sense of being right. A debater exerts mental energy and uses the power of the voice, not the strength or agility of the body.

It's a sport of the mind because you play to reach a higher standard. Better arguments. Better counter-arguments. Better style and structure. Like any sport, you can always outperform what you did previously. There's a tougher opponent out there who will challenge you to debate more effectively than you once thought possible. No case and no argument will ever be perfect. There's always something greater to achieve. A debater never says, "That's the best I can do."

It's a sport of the mind because you have to think on your feet as the game goes on. Like most sports, debate isn't predictable. Adaptation is the name of the game. You come into it prepared to argue your case. But you're equally prepared to change on the fly. You're ready to pounce on your opponent's weaknesses and to plug holes that have been infiltrated by your rivals. There are no 'cookie-cutter' templates, and no rigid formulas. It's a game with simple rules and general strategies for success. The rest is up to you.

In the sport of debate, your equipment is your voice. It's equipment that must be honed and optimized for success. But your voice alone will not make you a top debater. A golfer's drive is enhanced by his or her choice of clubs, not accomplished by the clubs alone. A hockey goalie's pads help to stop shots, but the real test is one of reflexes and anticipation. Similarly, a compelling voice can only enhance what your mind produces, but it's no substitute for great ideas.

As you strive to excel at debate, you'll make mistakes along the way. And don't be too hard on yourself when you do. Not even the world's leading debaters perform flawlessly. Debate isn't a science that you can perfect. Like any sport, if you fall, your best bet is to pick up the pieces and move on.

So put yourself into the mindset of a competitor, and get set to tackle the sport of debate!

CHAPTER 1

Get Ready:
Turn On the Power of Your Voice

Coming Up!

A strong, healthy voice allows you to speak clearly and effectively. This chapter will show you how to prepare your voice and body and how to control your nerves. It will also reveal practical techniques to help you keep your voice in tip-top shape.

GET SET TO SPEAK

Like an athlete who stretches before a game, preparing your voice, body, and mind is essential to producing strong and clear speech. Unfortunately, most people don't associate warming up with speech, which is why most speakers don't warm up at all. But those who want to give themselves a competitive edge don't miss this important step.

You're probably thinking that it would be rather awkward to warm up in front of other people. Thankfully, you can avoid being glared at as you get yourself ready to speak. Whether you warm up in the car, in an empty room, or at home, a few simple strategies and exercises will help you speak more comfortably and effectively:

> **Success Tip!**
>
> Before you speak, relax your mind and body.

Walk before you talk. One of the most effective ways to relax your mind and body is also the easiest. Before you speak, spend a few minutes walking slowly in a room or hallway. Imagine how fast you'll be talking, and 'match' it to your walking speed. Taking a walk will help you release any unnecessary tension and clear your mind of distractions. Think about how you'll walk to the front of the room and what you'll do to engage your audience. Briefly recall your introduction, main points, and conclusion.

Relax your body. Stress in your body makes it more difficult to speak clearly and expressively. Loosen your arms, shoulders, and legs in the same way you would if you were preparing for a run. This will make your voice more effective by freeing up any tension in your body. Your hand gestures and body language will also seem more natural.

Loosen your jaw. A strained jaw makes it more difficult to articulate and project your voice effectively. Good articulation helps you say words and phrases with clarity and precision. Strong projection helps you convey confidence and engage with the entire audience, including those seated at the back of the room. Before you speak, try dropping your jaw loosely several times. This will keep it flexible and free of strain when it's your turn to talk.

Take deep breaths. Breathing deeply before you start to speak will help you relax. It will also put you in a frame of mind to use deep breathing while you're speaking. This will allow your speech to flow more smoothly and naturally.

Try a few tongue twisters. Doing so will help get your articulators ready for clear communication. It's common to stumble over a few phrases when you deliver a speech. Going through a number of tongue twisters is one way to reduce how often this happens. To practice a variety of sounds, use a few of the tongue twisters listed below, repeating each one at least three times in a row:

Yellow yo-yo.	Wild winter wind.	Toy boat.
Blood red bed bugs.	Six selfish shellfish.	Knapsack straps.
Two tooth sleuths.	Hiccup teacup.	Sixish.
Shop sign shines.	Slapstick skit.	Truly rural.

Stay calm. Don't put added pressure on yourself. It will only make you more nervous before you speak and disappointed if you make errors. The best way to be ready to perform is getting into the right state of mind. If you tell yourself that you're going to succeed, you probably will. Most people are their own worst critics and get nervous before delivering a speech. Be an optimist, and you'll be measurably more comfortable when you speak in public.

COOL YOUR NERVES

In surveys, people often identify public speaking as one of their top fears, often ahead of heights and death! Even if you know everyone in the audience, it's not uncommon to have jitters before and while you speak. It's normal to be apprehensive about speaking, but how you deal with it is what makes all the difference. You want to appear confident and relaxed, which will improve the impression you make on your audience.

It's easy to tell when a speaker is nervous. Nervous speakers often shake, fidget, stiffen their bodies, or seem like they're simply trying to get through their speech. Although everyone deals with nervousness in a different way, there are a few simple techniques that you may find useful to help you become more comfortable:

Memorize the first few words. There's nothing more comforting than a great start. If you pull off the first line or two solidly, you'll feel that you have momentum as you continue with your speech. On the other hand, it's tough for many speakers to recover from stumbles in the opening phrases. Go into your speech knowing exactly what you're going to say at the start.

Success Tip!

Perfect your opening to give yourself early momentum.

Go through your introduction many times. In addition to memorizing the first line or two of your speech, it's also helpful to know how you'll *deliver* your introduction. The introduction sets the stage, both for you and for your audience. A solid, well-delivered introduction is a great 'icebreaker' into the rest of your speech. It gives you confidence right when you begin.

Know your content well. Nothing beats nervousness more effectively than being comfortable with your material. Understand your topic in detail, so that if you lose your place or have to answer questions, you can be confident that you know the necessary concepts.

Practice out loud. Whether you practice by yourself, at home in front of your family, or before a group of friends, verbalizing your points is a great way to reduce nervousness. You may even want to watch yourself in the mirror, so that you can see what others will be watching as you speak. Check that you're gesturing naturally, standing with confident posture, and using good facial expression. This will make you feel far more comfortable as you go into your speech.

Use pauses effectively. When you go to the front of the room, give yourself a moment to gather your thoughts and to establish a relaxed and confident stance. Rushing into your speech is a sure way to accentuate any nervousness. If you become nervous during your speech, don't apologize or fill in the space with the common "um" or "ah." Pause, get back your composure, gather your thoughts, and continue your speech with confidence.

Have confidence in yourself. If you tell yourself that you're going to do poorly, there's a very good chance that you will. Remind yourself that you know your speech and are confident in your ability. Not even professionals with decades of experience deliver perfect speeches, so you shouldn't pressure yourself to be perfect either.

KEEP YOUR VOICE IN TIP-TOP SHAPE

Imagine a skier racing with a broken pole, or a rower paddling with a split oar. How well would they do? Most likely, not well at all. Athletes in every sport have to keep their equipment in great shape if they want to perform up to their potential.

But what does any of this have to do with effective speech and debate? Actually, more than you may think. If you want your voice to produce clear, high-quality speech for your lifetime, it's essential that you take care of it. Building and sustaining a healthy voice requires you to pay attention to the following practices in your daily life:

> **Watch Out!**
>
> Avoid habits that strain your voice.

Avoid screaming and shouting. You may think that these common practices are harmless, spontaneous reactions to the world around us. The reality is that they put enormous strain on your vocal cords. Over time, they reduce the clarity of your speech and damage your voice, particularly the muscles that help you produce sound. If you want to protect your voice against unnecessary damage, keep your speech within a normal volume range.

Drink plenty of water. Not only will you improve your body's health, you'll also enhance your voice by keeping your mouth moist and reducing tension in your throat. Especially before a speech or debate, sipping water will improve the clarity of your voice when you speak.

Break the bad habits of clenching or grinding your jaw. In addition to your dentist's very wise advice, keeping your mouth relaxed for excellent speech communication is another reason to eliminate these unhealthy practices. Speakers and debaters need to manipulate their articulators in order to wrap themselves around some of their more sophisticated words and phrases. Avoiding these habits will make it easier for others to understand what you're saying.

Take in plenty of air. Air must flow freely and frequently in order for your voice to function at its highest possible quality. Taking plenty of pauses will help increase the air flow. And don't talk too fast, as doing so will only make it harder to get enough air.

Don't overuse your voice when you're sick or tired. Illness and fatigue can strain your vocal instruments. Over many years, talking excessively when your body is weak can be damaging. Limiting how much you talk while you're sick or tired will go a long way in reducing unnecessary harm to your voice.

Never clear your throat harshly. Doing so places unnecessary stress on your vocal cords. Eventually, your voice will be become less clear and less pleasing to the listener. Drinking water, swallowing, or coughing gently are all appropriate alternatives.

If you follow the tips discussed in this chapter, you'll enhance the quality of your speech, and you'll feel more prepared and confident when it's your turn to talk.

Chapter 1: Keys to Success

✔ **Warm up before you speak.** You'll help prepare your voice for exceptional verbal communication and your body for effective non-verbal communication. In addition, you'll put your mind in a more comfortable, relaxed mood, which will help you speak more smoothly and naturally.

✔ **Keep your nerves in check.** It's natural to be nervous, but it's easy to fix. Placing yourself in the right state of mind will help you overcome any jitters you may have. Even if you're slightly nervous, don't make it obvious to your audience.

✔ **Maintain a healthy voice.** Similar to how injuries to your body make it tough for you to excel at sports, straining your voice makes it harder for you to perform at your peak when speaking and debating. Avoid bad habits that hurt the clarity and expressiveness of your voice.

CHAPTER 2

Lift Off:
Great Games to Get You Started

Coming Up!

It often takes a quick and enjoyable warm up to get your mind ready for speech and debate. This section will tell you about a few games and exercises that will help prepare you to speak. These activities will also introduce you to some common speech and debate techniques.

NOT YOUR TYPICAL 'BORED' GAMES

In addition to warming up and practicing your vocal skills, there are a number of games and exercises that will gear up your mind for speech and debate. Some of these activities, such as *Rapid Speak* and *Pass the Baton*, can be done with two or three people. Others, such as *Crossfire* and *On That Point*, require a larger group. You're encouraged to adapt these games to your specific situation, including the number of people in your group and how much time you have.

Success Tip!

Play a game at the beginning of a practice session.

Rapid Speak

The main purpose of this game is to allow you to practice speaking without preparation, also known as impromptu speaking. It will encourage you to use effective transitions, which will help make your phrasing smoother. Here's how *Rapid Speak* works:

• *Step #1: Chairperson with cards.* A Chairperson has a stack of 30 to 40 cards, each of which has a random word that the participant must incorporate into his or her speech.

• *Step #2: Participant starts to speak.* The Chairperson shows a randomly selected word to the participant, who must then start a speech on that subject or on a related area.

• *Step #3: Flipping to new words.* The Chairperson flips to a new word every 15 seconds, at which point the speaker has to make a logical transition to the new subject. Each speaker goes through 12 words, or approximately three minutes of speech.

You'll probably end up with a rather creative and humorous speech, especially considering the random nature of the word selection. It's okay for you to take some time when transitioning to the new point. Here's a condensed example of *Rapid Speak*:

"[Pizza] Yesterday evening, I went out for pizza with my family. My younger brother had the misfortune of spilling his pop all over the table which, sadly, did not come as a surprise. My parents told him [School] that he would get a detention if he did that sort of thing at school, but of course my brother tends not to listen to anything. Last week, he got into trouble for spitting at another student [Music] in the middle of his music class."

Crossfire

This game allows you to participate in a dynamic, back and forth debate without having to deliver a lengthy explanation for each argument. It forces you to come up with points on the spot—a key skill in debate. *Crossfire* also gets you used to debating both sides of an issue, which you'll have to do in a debate tournament. Here's how it works:

• *Step #1: Form teams.* At the front of the room, split into two lines: one side arguing for the topic and the other side arguing against it.

• *Step #2: Set the debate.* The students at the front of the lines should be facing each other at the center of the room. A Chairperson then presents a statement for debate.

• *Step #4: Point in favor.* The first speaker in favor of the statement speaks for 15 to 30 seconds and moves to the back of the other line.

• *Step #5: Point against.* The first speaker against the topic speaks for 15 to 30 seconds and moves to the back of the other line.

• *Step #6: Continue the debate.* The back and forth process continues until every debater has spoken at least once for both sides.

Each time it's your turn, limit yourself to one clear point. It can be a new argument or opposition to an argument made by the other side. Make sure to keep the debate flowing, as the goal is to form and respond to arguments quickly.

On That Point

This game allows two participants to work together as they represent a perspective, while everyone else gets practice asking challenging questions. It's particularly good practice for parliamentary debate, which allows seated debaters to ask questions to the person speaking. *On That Point* operates according to the following procedures:

• *Step #1: Get into teams.* Two participants go to the front of the room to argue for an opinion statement of their choice. Everyone else is in the audience, which forms the team debating against this statement.

• *Step #2: Two speakers start.* The two debaters arguing in favor of the statement talk one at a time. Only the person holding the baton can speak. When the debater who has the floor passes the baton to his or her teammate, this individual continues the debate.

• *Step #3: "On that Point."* Anyone from the audience can stand up at any time and say, "On that point" and ask a critical question to the two debaters. The game goes on for up to 10 minutes.

It's important that the audience strikes a good balance between asking enough questions and not bombarding the two debaters with too many questions. Allow the speaker to complete the answer and to continue the speech before asking another question. Below is an excerpt from a sample game of *On That Point* on the topic, "Students have a right to privacy in schools."

Speaker #1: "A student's locker should be a private space to store possessions. We wouldn't allow police to search arbitrarily the bedrooms of students at their homes. Likewise, what a student keeps in a locker is nobody else's business."

Audience Member A: "On that point! But when students enter a school, aren't they entering a public space, subject to the rules and regulations of that particular institution?"

Speaker #1: "Certainly, what they do in classrooms and hallways should be governed by the school's rules. But the very nature of a locker—a *closed, locked* area—makes it a student's private area." (Baton gets passed to partner.)

Speaker #2: "Not only that, but allowing school officials to search students' lockers is a system that's very prone to abuse. In particular, there's no formal warrant process, and no legal justification is ever required before a search is conducted. This leaves students wondering whether they can trust school officials."

Audience Member B: "On That Point, sir. Don't you think that school officials have a responsibility to ensure that drugs, weapons, and other banned items aren't brought to school?"

Pass the Baton

Pass the Baton aims for the type of back and forth flow seen in *Crossfire*, but it takes place as a group discussion rather than as a head to head battle. It gives you virtually no time to prepare an argument, which serves as a true test of debating skills. The game involves the following steps:

> **Watch Out!**
>
> When playing debate games, be careful not to get off topic.

• *Step #1: Start the debate.* Everyone in the group stands in a circle and jointly selects a topic for debate. One person, who holds the baton, begins the debate by making an argument in favor of the statement.

• *Step #2: The next person opposes.* Once the first speaker has finished making a single argument, the baton gets passed to any other person in the circle. This participant must oppose what the first speaker has said, either directly or with a new argument.

• *Step #3: The debate continues.* The second speaker passes the baton to another participant, and the process continues until each person has spoken two to three times.

You won't know when you'll be called to speak or what side you'll be arguing. It's essential that you listen carefully to the flow of the discussion and anticipate what you would do if you had to speak next. This dynamic and lively game is sure to keep you on your toes. Below is a selection from a sample *Pass the Baton* game on the subject, "Museums and theatres should fund themselves."

Participant #1 (in favor): "If people truly want museums and theatres, they should be willing to pay for them. Why should the public subsidize someone's *personal* entertainment?" (Baton gets passed on.)

Participant #2 (opposed): "However, let's not forget that museums and theatres are good for the public as a whole. We all benefit when we preserve and enhance our culture." (Baton gets passed on.)

Participant #3 (in favor): "Well, not everyone benefits equally. We each have likes and dislikes. There's no vote to determine whether an art institution gets public funding. Let the people decide with their wallets!" (Baton gets passed on.)

Participant #4 (opposed): "You're basing your argument on the idea that museums and theatres should all be commercial, for-profit operations. I believe that they shouldn't be run exactly the same way as private companies. They're supposed to serve society as a whole, not just the business interests of an owner."

Traffic Lights

The purpose of this game is to give every participant a chance to speak three times, each time for a distinct purpose. You'll either have to make a point, raise a concern, or refute a point made by another participant. You get to decide when you want to speak, what side you want to take, and how to argue for the perspective of your choice. *Traffic Lights* runs according to the following rules:

• *Step #1: Cards get distributed.* Every member of the group has a green card, a yellow card, and a red card. Each card can be used only once in the debate, and cards cannot be traded between players. To talk, you must use the appropriate card:

> *Green is Go:* Make a new argument that adds to the debate.
> *Yellow is Caution:* Raise a concern or question you want addressed.
> *Red is Stop:* Oppose the argument that has just been presented.

• *Step #2: Anyone begins the debate.* The first person to use a green card starts the debate. A green card guarantees the person using it at least 30 seconds of uninterrupted time.

• *Step #3: Another person interjects.* After this 30 second period has expired, anyone else can use a card. A green card guarantees a fresh 30 second period, a yellow card 15 seconds to ask a question, and a red card 30 seconds to oppose the point made previously. If either a yellow card or a red card is used, the original speaker gets to continue thereafter until someone else uses a card.

• *Step #4: The debate continues. Traffic Lights* continues until every participant is out of cards. This means that everyone will have raised an argument, opposed an argument, and asked a question, all of which are important debating skills.

Debate Duel

Debate Duel allows you to go head to head against other competitors, spicing up the debate with some heated rivalry. Your goal is to survive the battles as long as you can by continuing to win mini-debates against different opponents. But your fate lies in the hands of your peers. Here's how to play *Debate Duel*:

• *Step #1: Take your positions.* There are two debaters standing at the front of the room facing each other: the Champion and the Challenger. Everyone else sits in the audience and makes up the Jury. The Jury must act objectively. Alternatively, you can opt for an independent Jury that doesn't participate in the debate.

• *Step #2: Begin the battle.* The Champion, who is selected randomly for the first round, gets 30 seconds to present an argument on any topic of his or her choice. The Challenger then gets 30 seconds to present a counter-argument.

• *Step #3: The Jury votes.* After both people have their say, the Jury, by a majority vote, eliminates the debater it believes lost the duel. The person left is the Champion, and the participant voted off becomes a member of the Jury.

• *Step #4: A new Challenger emerges.* According to a pre-set order, a member of the Jury then takes the position of Challenger, and the process starts again. The person who has the longest consecutive run as the Champion wins the game.

The Great Race

This game pits teams against each other in a battle of quick thinking, which is great practice for the fast-paced world of competitive debating. Hesitation will cost you dearly. Here's how *The Great Race* works:

• *Step #1: Get into two teams.* Half of the participants form one team and stand on one side of the room, and the rest of the participants face them and make up the other team.

• *Step #2: Prepare for the race.* In between the teams, there's a table with a buzzer or bell. A member from each team stands on either side of the table. Both competitors must have their hands behind their backs.

• *Step #3: The race is on.* The Chairperson announces a statement for debate. The first person to ring the buzzer or bell has to make an argument in favor of the statement, which should last for approximately 10 seconds. The team represented by this participant scores a point. If, however, the speaker waits or hesitates, or if the Chairperson decides that the argument isn't a valid point, the other team scores a point.

• *Step #4: The sprint continues.* After each round, a new person takes the position at the table. Keep on playing the game until each person has spoken at least once, or twice if there are only a few participants.

Survivor

Survivor is a 'winner takes all' competition in which every debater tries to outlast everyone else by presenting the strongest arguments. To win at *Survivor*, you have to perform well round after round, or else you may get voted off the Island. Here's how to play the game:

• *Step #1: All aboard the Island.* The Contenders stand in a group at the front of the room. The Jury sits in the audience, which consists only of the Chairperson at this point.

• *Step #2: The round begins.* The Chairperson announces a topic, and every debater has to present an argument of approximately 15 seconds for or against this statement.

• *Step #3: Someone gets voted off.* Each member of the Jury—one person in the first round—casts a vote for the debater whose argument seemed the weakest. The person who gets the most votes is eliminated from the Island and joins the Jury. In the event of a tie, the Chairperson casts the deciding vote.

• *Step #4: Battle to the end.* After each round, the Jury pool will increase by one member and the Contender group will decrease by one member. Keep on playing the game until only one Contender, the 'Survivor', is left standing.

The games and exercises discussed in this chapter are a few of the ways that you can get into the right frame of mind for effective debating and public speaking. They're lively and enjoyable, making them great activities for a group of people.

Chapter 2: Keys to Success

✔ **Listen to the back and forth flow of arguments**. Understanding how the arguments shift from side to side is central to grasping the debate. Equally important, pay attention to what causes an argument to go off topic, so that you can avoid such situations when you debate.

✔ **Think about how you would expand on the points**. Most of the games require very brief arguments. In an actual debate, you would have to expand these brief arguments into more complete points by adding explanations and details.

✔ **Be fully involved**. If you're a beginner, these games will help you get comfortable making arguments. Even if you have significant experience, they'll keep your skills sharp and provide great ways to warm up before you debate.

✔ **Enjoy yourself**. You'll find that these games often get rather lighthearted and humorous, which is why they're great for warming up and practicing. So don't analyze your performance too critically. Enjoy the games, particularly the interaction with your fellow participants.

SPEECH SAVVY:
DAZZLE WITH A DYNAMIC STYLE

Part II

CHAPTER 3

What You Say:
Ingredients of Intelligent Speaking

Coming Up!

The first step toward mastering speech and debate is to know how to build an interesting, relevant, and effective speech. This chapter will show you how to zero-in on your primary purpose and how to develop and structure your key points.

WHAT'S YOUR POINT?

Greek philosopher Aristotle once said, "A speech has two parts. You must state your case, and you must prove it." At its core, this is what a speech boils down to. Sounds simple? Well, it isn't.

Before you start to develop your speech, you need to know what exactly you're trying to accomplish. It's important to make your speech relevant to the specific issue or situation. Avoid trying to say anything and everything about the subject. Instead, focus on a few main ideas and explain them clearly and completely.

> **Did You Know?**
>
> A British lawyer once delivered a speech that lasted 119 days.

Speeches are generally intended to *inform*, to *persuade*, or to *entertain*. You may find it necessary to combine the techniques of more than one of these types of speeches. For instance, many persuasive speeches have heavy informative content as a way of laying the foundation for the main arguments. And some of the most captivating speakers inject humor into their speeches. Ultimately, you have to consider your topic, your intent, and your environment.

In the Know: Informative Speeches

When speaking to inform, your main objective is to explain, detail, instruct, or clarify. In this type of speech, the precision and clarity of your ideas are critically important, because you're trying to help your audience understand the issue. Given the nature of an informative speech, it's tempting to overload your listeners with facts and details. Avoid this tendency as much as possible. The information you present is only useful to the extent that it's *absorbed* and *remembered*. Informative speaking skills will help you greatly in debating, particularly when you have to present evidence and clearly explain concepts to your judges. Here are a few examples of informative speech topics:

- The Internet's impact on education and research.
- Changes to the school disciplinary policy.
- United Nations peacekeeping involvement.
- Developments in natural, alternative medicines.
- New frontiers in science and technology research.

The Sales Pitch: Persuasive Speeches

Your ability to deliver persuasive speeches is essential to debating. The purpose is to convince your audience about a set of values or proposals and, in some cases, to inspire or compel a group to take action. An example of persuasive speaking you'll be familiar with is a campaign speech for student government. Important attributes for this type of speaking include a set of strong arguments, a convincing tone, and a passionate style of delivery. If you want to convince others to agree with your arguments, it's vital that you speak with conviction. Here are a few examples of persuasive speech topics:

- The military should receive more funding.
- Standardized tests should be phased out.
- Space exploration should be stopped.
- School uniforms should be eliminated.
- Voting should be mandatory.

Make Them Laugh: Entertaining Speeches

A speech to entertain will most commonly be delivered as a special occasion speech, such as an after dinner speech or a comedy routine during a talent show. In some instances, you may have a persuasive intent, such as using humor to mock a policy. You'll typically use entertaining speaking strategies so that your speech to inform or persuade will become more interesting. To be entertaining, your entire speech need not be funny or on a humorous topic. In fact, using witty words or a lighthearted and humorous style can be equally effective. Even the most serious arguments can be illustrated using humor.

GET TO THE POINT: YOUR MAIN IDEA

Prior to deciding on your key points, write a sentence that summarizes your speech's general idea. This topic sentence should be your focus when you build the content of your speech. You're much more effective when you focus on the core of your ideas than when you jump around from topic

Watch Out!

Avoid making broad, unfocused speeches.

to topic without a strong connection between points. Considering that you have limited time, you should include only a few, well-developed points in your speech.

CHURN OUT THE POINTS

Once you've identified your purpose and your overall theme, the next step is to find three to five main points that you want to talk about. Less than three seems too 'bare', and more than five seems too 'busy'. Begin this brainstorming process using a list or a mind map. Include everything you know about the topic, even if you don't immediately think it's relevant or important.

In a short period of time, you'll likely find many different points that you want to discuss. Your next step is to narrow down your speech to a few key ideas. One rule of thumb is to use the 3S system, or *Sort, Select*, and *Summarize*:

1. **Sort similar ideas together**. You may have listed several points that can be added as details and explanations for a larger idea.

2. **Select only the most essential topics**. It's much more effective to focus on your primary purpose than to ramble into unrelated ideas that decrease the overall impact of your speech.

3. **Summarize each topic with a title**. After you're down to three to five points, a brief heading for each one will help you find details and will enable you to focus your explanations.

BREAK IT DOWN: STRUCTURING YOUR SPEECH

Once you've come up with your main ideas, the next step is to organize your speech for maximum effectiveness. Speech organization isn't difficult, but it is very important. It makes your speech clearer and your ideas easier to remember. The basic organization for any speech, either on its own or in a debate, is an introduction, three or four content sections, and a conclusion.

Success Tip!

Match your structure to your subject.

There are many different ways to break down your key ideas. Which method you select depends in large part on the type and topic of your speech. It's important for you to think carefully about how you want to organize your points, because your structure can make or break how easily the audience is able to grasp what you're saying. Here are some of the ways to structure your points:

Topics and Themes. This is the most common way to organize a speech. The idea is to divide your points into different subject areas and to focus each point on a single topic. A common pitfall is that the subject areas are overly distinct, making the speech seem disjointed. Be sure that one area leads smoothly into the next by selecting and ordering the themes in a logical manner. Here's an example of organization by topic for a speech explaining how media organizations have a social responsibility:

• Point #1: *The media provides vital alerts.* You could talk about advisories during natural disasters and alerts of missing children. Making this point your first one is logical, because by clearly explaining a critical function, it sets the tone for your overall message.

• Point #2: *The media educates us on important matters.* Here, you could discuss media reporting of health issues, safety tips, faulty consumer products, and other matters important to our daily lives. It's a logical extension from the first point, because it deals with media functions that are critical to us personally. But it's different enough from the first point, as its focus is on less urgent matters.

• Point #3: *The media keeps us informed about current affairs.* This section could focus on our desire to be informed about national political affairs, global politics, sports, and other day to day events. This point extends logically from the second point. It's similar in its focus on matters of daily importance, but it's different in its emphasis on information that's not as essential.

Time and Progression. Chronological organization is often the easiest for the audience to follow. People naturally think in terms of time. For example, what do I need to do in the morning, then in the afternoon, and then in the evening? Extending this logic to speech, organizing by time allows you to lead your audience on an easy to understand progression. Below is an example of time-based organization for a speech outlining how the local government could encourage recycling:

• Point #1: *Make it easy for people to recycle.* You could suggest that regular pickups and free recycling boxes divided into categories of materials is the first step in encouraging more recycling. If it's not convenient, nothing else is likely to work.

• Point #2: *A campaign to motivate people to recycle more.* Once you've made it convenient to recycle, a logical next step is to tell them why they should even bother. A television advertising or direct mail campaign could be part of this section.

• Point #3: *A long-term strategy to inform the public.* Now that you've encouraged people to recycle more, how do you make sure that they continue to do so in the long-term? Of course, continuing to make it convenient and advertising that they should recycle could be part of the strategy. But you could say that the next major step is to tell the public about the positive results of its cooperation.

Physical Location. Many people organize their thoughts according to where items are or where situations occur. The same tool can be applied to speech topics, particularly when there are multiple events or circumstances happening in different areas. Say you're talking about solutions to poverty in various parts of the world:

• Point #1: *Improving government systems in Africa.* You could argue that building democratic and transparent government institutions is the first step in alleviating poverty in Africa. The incentives of debt relief and aid could be used to push forward these reforms.

• Point #2: *Reforming economic systems in Latin America.* Economic and currency instability in many parts of Latin America could be cited as problems in need of action.

• Point #3: *Building infrastructure in South Asia.* You could make the case that the large, but mostly poor populations of South Asia would benefit from infrastructure investment. Development of roads, schools, hospitals, and sanitation systems could be touted as solutions.

Problem and Solution. This organizational method is great if a problem isn't widely accepted or understood, and if you're trying to establish the problem as the basis for a solution. It's important that your solution closely matches and directly addresses the problems. Here's an example of this type of speech structure if you're arguing that pharmaceutical companies should have to make more of the data from clinical trials available to the public:

• *Point #1: Problem of medical side-effects.* Explain the extent to which drugs approved by government agencies are later found to pose serious health risks. In particular, you could use well-publicized examples of drugs which were released and later discovered to cause health ailments, including severe illnesses and deaths.

• *Point #2: Problem of insufficient information.* You could argue that without full information from all clinical trials, medical professionals and members of the public don't have enough of an ability to scrutinize drugs and make their own judgments.

• *Point #3: Solution of more public information.* Your solution could be that pharmaceutical companies should have to release more information to the public. The immediate result would be at least a partial solution to the problem of insufficient information. Then, you could argue that if this problem is solved and there is greater public scrutiny of drugs, the result would be fewer medical side-effects.

Building the Pieces: Structuring Each Point

Like each paragraph in an essay, each section in a speech needs to have a sound structure. A general rule to remember is to "Claim, Comment, Cite, and Conclude" for each section:

1. **Claim** your point, usually in a single sentence. This serves as a 'signpost' to your audience members, setting the stage for what you're hoping to explain to them. You want your listeners to be thinking to themselves, "Okay, we're on a new point now, and that's precisely what the point is about. Let's see what the speaker has to say about it." An example of claiming your point is, "My second point is that if genetically-modified foods are sold without appropriate labeling, it reduces the confidence that people have in the food supply."

31

2. **Comment** on the point, presenting important analysis and logic. Explain in greater depth what the point means, or why it's correct. Using the previous example, you could say, "Everyone wants to feel certainty and security when they pick up food from the grocery store. If they don't have sufficient information ..."

3. **Cite** different pieces of evidence to support your underlying claims. This essentially tells your audience, "Don't just take my word for it. There are facts that support what I'm saying." Continuing with the issue of genetically-modified foods, you could state, "The percent of genetically-modified foods labeled as such is very low, especially when compared to the percent of people who want to know this information. It's been found that ..."

4. **Conclude** the section either by restating the main point in different words or by explaining the importance of the point to the main idea of the speech. For example, "Therefore, it's clear that the absence of standard and enforceable labeling requirements has caused unacceptable harm to public confidence in food products."

Completing the Puzzle: Overall Organization

The order in which you present your content sections is largely a matter of judgment and personal preference. Many speakers will start and finish with their most important ideas. However, particularly in persuasive speeches, you may want to build your points into a final idea that proves your overall theme.

Most audience members have great difficulty remembering a point the first time they hear it. As the speaker, it makes perfect sense to you, but your audience usually needs reminders. Many communicators fail to guide their listeners. They only briefly summarize their speech, out of fear that they're simply repeating themselves. Well, repetition works. Most of what we learn is repeated to us several times, although often in different forms and styles. Here's a great framework for making your speech organized and your points easier for the audience members to remember:

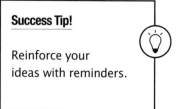

Success Tip!

Reinforce your
ideas with reminders.

1. **"Tell them what you're going to tell them."** Paint a road map for the audience. At minimum, tell them in general terms what they can expect to hear from you. A speech isn't a mystery novel. If you want to capture interest and create understanding, tell your listeners what path you'll be taking with your speech.

2. **"Tell them."** This section includes the three to five main points of your speech. They must be distinct sections with smooth transitions and logical ordering. In this part, you convey the 'meat' of your speech—the points and supporting details that deliver your message.

3. **"Tell them what you told them."** Huh? But didn't you already tell them? Actually, the most effective speakers remind the audience of their key points. The conclusion should tie the entire speech together, taking a variety of points and summarizing them around your core theme. Your audience will remember much more of your speech if you do a point by point summary.

SEARCHING FOR SUPPORT

After you have an overall skeleton of your speech, namely three to five main points, you're ready to find the details necessary to be effective. There are many places you can look to find this information, which are likely the same places you would go if you were writing an essay. Below are some of the places to search for details:

> **Success Tip!**
>
> Stay on top of what's happening in the news.

Libraries will likely have information on your subject. It's now easier than ever to find what you're looking for, because most libraries have electronic search databases. You'll also want to look in encyclopedias and other reference works for any relevant details.

The Internet is the fastest and easiest way to find current information on virtually any subject. Unfortunately, it's also filled with many unreliable sources, so you'll have to use your good sense and critical judgment to separate fact from fiction.

Family and friends who work in a field related to your speech topic, or who you feel would have significant knowledge about your subject, are always excellent resources to contact.

PROVING THE POINTS

Many different types of evidence can be useful in both informative and persuasive speeches. These include statistics, events, quotations, reports, and analogies, to name a few. You should use one or two pieces of evidence to support each of your points, along with clear explanations of how the evidence proves what you're saying.

Flaunting the Facts

Statistics are typically anything to do with numbers. Your statistics should come from reliable sources. For instance, the audience members are more likely to believe facts from a study by a well-respected university than from a special interest group that they've never heard of before (not to mention that the group may appear biased). Be careful not to overuse statistics, because unless you're speaking to a group of academics, the audience will likely get quite bored. If used correctly, however, statistics and reports can add significant credibility, depth, and clarity to your main ideas.

For example: How many people died from cancer over the last year? How much money does it cost to provide prescription drug benefits to every one of the country's senior citizens? What percent of the city's teenagers use illegal drugs?

Making it Real

True events, stories, and comparisons are some of the examples you may want to include in order to enhance your speech. They show that an action or circumstance actually did happen or is taking place currently, lending credibility to your main ideas. And they're effective at simplifying or clarifying your position. If you want to use a hypothetical event or story, make sure it's realistic, or else it won't add any real value. A comparison can be useful in drawing clear distinctions, helping to illustrate your points. Here are some of the speech topics for which an event, story, or comparison may be effective:

• **Drunk driving**: If trying to prove the detrimental impact that drunk drivers have on society, it could be useful to talk about a recent and local tragedy, and how it changed life for the victim's family.

• **Land mines**: If your objective is to debate in favor of banning the production and sale of land mines, try describing the story of a child who was a victim of a land mine explosion.

• **Post-secondary education**: A career, lifestyle, and salary comparison of a student with post-secondary education to a student with only a high school diploma could be an effective way to prove the value of continuing education past high school.

Evoking the Experts

Used properly, quotations from famous people or experts in the field can be valuable additions to your speech. For example, if your speech is about freedom and civil rights, you could quote from Martin Luther King Jr.'s "I Have a Dream" speech. When considering the use of a quotation, make sure it adds substance, not just an endorsement. And don't overuse quotations, because they reflect someone's opinion rather than conclusive evidence.

INTRIGUING INTRODUCTIONS

The first 30 to 40 seconds of your speech are in many respects the most important, because they give you an opportunity to capture the audience's attention. It's your way of saying, "Listen to what I have to say," as well as establishing your main idea and outlining your structure. Start with something that grabs attention, such as a startling statistic, a rhetorical question, an appeal to emotion, or a humorous story. Here are some examples of attention-grabbing introductions:

> **Success Tip!**
>
> To make an emotional connection, use vivid language.

• **Startling Statistics**: "Last year alone, 49 people in this city were murdered. Out of this alarming number, 38 were innocent civilians, and 11 of them were children."

• **Rhetorical Questions**: "Do you feel unsafe these days? Are you afraid to walk outside at night? Do you now fear for the safety of your young children when they play in the front yard or go to school?"

• **Appeal to Emotion**: "The criminals are winning the battle against us, the law-abiding citizens of this city. Too many of us are innocent victims of criminals, many of whom are getting away with violence because of lax policing. Ladies and gentlemen, I say it's time for change. It's time for our government to pour in the resources necessary to make our streets safer for all of us."

• **Humorous Story**: "Lady Astor once said to Winston Churchill, 'Winston, if I were your wife I'd put poison in your coffee'. You would expect the recipient of such a personal attack to be rather phased and quite angry. But in classic Churchillian fashion, he instead quipped back, 'Nancy, if I were your husband I'd drink it.'"

There are many different ways to organize your speech's introduction. However, there's no perfect structure. It's important that you try a variety of styles and formats. To get you started, here's one example of a format for your opening:

Step #1: Grab the audience's attention. As mentioned previously, the most effective introductions start with a 'hook' that encourages the audience members to listen to what you have to say. This attention-grabber usually hints at the topic or theme of your speech.

Step #2: Address the audience. Always acknowledge your audience. For example, you could say, "Ladies and gentlemen …" or "Mr. Chairperson, judges, and worthy opponents …" Unfortunately, many people spend too long on this part, presenting a laundry list of people in the audience. There's no need to take up time saying, for instance, "Teachers, parents, fellow students, school administrators, elected officials, alumni, and most welcome guests."

Step #3: State the topic of your speech. Make it very clear for your audience exactly what you're speaking about. Even if the audience knows the general topic, it's a good idea to narrow it down to a more concrete subject in order to provide a sense of focus to your speech.

Step #4: State your main idea or perspective. A speech isn't a drama. You shouldn't be leaving your listeners in suspense, hoping that they 'get it' by the end. State clearly and concisely what you hope to accomplish. This way, when people are listening, they'll know that your points are contributing toward your main idea.

Step #5: Outline the three to five main points of your speech. Many listeners find it helpful to know what, in general, the points will be. This makes it easier for them to follow your speech as you go along.

CATCHY CONCLUSIONS

Your conclusion depends largely on the purpose of your speech. The intent of the closing could be a call to action, a wrap up of your arguments, a summary of your informative points, a link back to your introduction, or a combination of these methods.

While your introduction catches the audience's attention, the conclusion is the final 'sales pitch' for your content and a reminder of your speech's main points. For example, if you're speaking in favor of more funding to fight global poverty, you may have opened your speech by describing the image of a starving child in Somalia. You could conclude by summarizing the reasons for more international development aid, reiterating how everyone can take local action to meet this objective, and finally, presenting the image of the young child in Somalia being given hope for a better life. Whatever you decide, make sure that you leave your audience with a memorable statement through which they can identify and think positively about your speech.

> **Watch Out!**
>
> Don't 'repeat' your introduction in your conclusion.

When you're moving into your conclusion, make sure that your audience knows you're doing so. While the simplest way is to say, "In conclusion," there are other methods as well. Saying, for example, "So what have I discussed today?" or "This speech essentially comes down to one overarching theme ..." will give your audience a cue that you're moving into the final part of your speech.

SMOOTH AND SIMPLE TRANSITIONS

When moving from section to section, you need a 'glue' to hold the speech together. Rather than shifting abruptly between points, tie your ideas together to create a sense of flow.

In persuasive speeches, effective transitions can tie directly into the building of arguments. For informative speeches, it may be more difficult to find this connection. Instead, you may want to start a section simply by saying that you're moving on to the next point, while referring to the previous point. Here are a few examples:

• *Speech to Persuade*: "Now that I've proven the brutal nature of capital punishment, I will show you how it's a violation of a citizen's most basic constitutional rights."

• *Speech to Inform*: "Not only has space exploration become less expensive, it's now much safer for our astronauts because of recent advances in shuttle technology."

As this chapter has discussed, having strong themes, points, and details combined with a carefully planned structure lays the foundation for an effective speech. It's important to be selective and methodical in deciding what ideas you want to get across to your audience.

Chapter 3: Keys to Success

✔ **A great speech is based on a unifying theme**. Even if they don't remember all of the details, your audience members should remember this main idea. Make sure that all of your points relate to this theme so that your speech stays on topic.

✔ **Develop possible points by brainstorming, and then place these ideas into categories**. You'll find that your initial list of ideas contains points that are closely related and can be grouped together. Also, you may find that some points overlap or don't relate directly to the theme. Use this process to narrow your speech down to a core set of points.

✔ **Research details to support your key points**. Including evidence, such as examples and statistics, adds credibility to your speech. In addition, evidence helps illustrate and enhance your points, making them clearer and stronger.

✔ **"Claim, Comment, Cite, and Conclude" for each point**. Begin with a clear statement of your point. Then, explain your point in greater depth. Move on by using evidence to support the explanations. Finally, conclude and tie the point into the 'big picture' or theme of your speech. This method will improve the structure and completeness of your key ideas.

✔ **"Tell them what you're going to tell them, then tell them, and then tell them what you told them."** Start your speech by laying out a 'road map' of what you intend to accomplish. Continue with the 'meat' of your speech, namely the main points and details. To conclude, reiterate your main points and show how they've proven the theme. Most people need reminders in order to understand fully what you've said.

✔ **Transition smoothly between points**. Your speech shouldn't be seen as isolated chunks of information. Rather, it should be seen as a connected set of ideas. Good transitions make it clear what you've accomplished and where you're going next.

CHAPTER 4

How You Say It:
Delivering with Poise and Pizzazz

Coming Up!

Once you've planned a great speech, the next step is delivering it effectively. In this chapter, you'll learn about different speech delivery styles, tools for verbal and non-verbal communication, how to mask mistakes, and ways of adapting to your audience.

THE "WOW!" FACTOR

You've probably been told not to judge a book by its cover. Do you actually listen to that advice? More likely than not, you decide to purchase, borrow, or read a book after looking at the cover, scanning the table of contents, and flipping quickly through the rest of it.

The same idea holds true for speech and debate. Many students spend hours developing exceptional content, only to deliver their speeches without making an impact. Most people hear others talking for hours each day, whether it be teachers, parents, or students. Do you listen attentively every single time someone is speaking? Probably not. You're naturally drawn toward clear, convincing, and interesting speakers. For these reasons, it's well worth your while to learn and practice the tools for excellent speech delivery.

THE RIGHT WAY TO WRITE IT

How you write down your speech (if at all) will have a significant impact on how well you deliver it. We each have our own style and preferences, so there's no 'one size fits all' method. However, there are clear advantages to selecting certain methods and disadvantages to going with others. Below is a discussion of the different ways to deliver a speech: *Outline, Script, Memorized,* and *Impromptu.*

Bare Bones: Outline Speaking

This type of speaking involves the use of an outline containing your main points. Although key phrases and parts of the introduction and conclusion may be written down word for word, the speaker must know all of the information well enough to speak naturally and clearly. Most successful speakers use an outline, because it allows for maximum fluency and ease of delivery.

Success Tip!

Use an outline rather than a script.

Some speakers write down only five or six lines as reminders of their main points. Others include details under each point. Take a look at the speech outlines on the next page to get a feel for this method.

OUTLINE SPEAKING: STANDARD

The most basic, easy to prepare method of speaking with an outline is to represent each point in with a single line:

    1. This reminds you what to talk about next.

    2. It allows you to maximize your eye contact.

    3. It also helps you speak more freely and naturally.

    4. And it shows you your speech's order 'at a glance'.

Of course, you could also go into more detail. For example:

    1. This reminds you what to talk about next.

        a. Most of us need these types of reminders.

        b. A single line can help you recall several ideas.

OUTLINE SPEAKING: VISUAL

Some of us prefer a more visual method. ↓

This doesn't provide very much detail. ↓

But it's a very clear, 'at a glance' outline tool. ↓

It's essentially a 'road map' of your speech.

SCRIPT SPEAKING: STANDARD

If you're not looking to do anything too creative with your script, bolding the first few words of every sentence will help you see your next line quickly and easily. **And if you've practiced** your speech a number of times, you may know what the entire line is from glancing at the first few words, allowing you to maintain strong eye contact. **It's also a good idea** to '1.5 space' your writing so that it's even easier to find your place. **Below you'll see** a line that helps you transition to the next page without creating an awkward pause as you turn the page.

2 / There is, though, a more creative ...

SCRIPT SPEAKING: CREATIVE

There is, though, a more creative approach. It takes *longer to prepare* and involves *more page turning*, but it's a great way to make your delivery **expressive** and **engaging**.

You can bold the first words of every sentence to help you *find your place*, and **you can bold** some of the other key words to **signal** that they should be emphasized. *Italicizing select words* also adds emphasis.

Laying out your speech in this staggered way, *one sentence per paragraph*, helps you **find your place** even faster.

Put it on Paper: Script Speaking

If you're a beginner at speech and debate, or if it's essential that every phrase be very accurate, you may want to consider a script. In this style of speaking, you write down your entire speech word for word, and you use the script for delivery. You should try to make eye contact with the audience as much as possible. If you don't, it will seem like you're talking to the *paper* more than you're communicating and engaging with the *audience*. Although script speaking may initially seem easier, it's less effective in terms of fluency and audience interest. Try switching to the outline style as soon as possible.

If speaking with a script, '1.5 space' your writing so that it's easier to find your place as you present. Write down your most important phrases and main points in bold font, underlined, or italicized so that these key lines stand out. Take a look at the examples on the previous page to see two ways of writing down a speech word for word.

Keep it in Mind: Memorized Speaking

If you have a photographic memory or too much time on your hands, you may want to consider memorizing your speech. Don't meet any of the above criteria? You're not alone! Memorized speaking isn't recommended for most people. Not only is this method difficult, but it also makes you seem less natural and relaxed. Your audience will likely be able to tell that you're struggling to remember each exact word.

Although memorizing an entire speech is fraught with problems, you may want to memorize the most important lines. For instance, if you have a few lines that you hope will stand out, saying them by heart may help you focus on making a connection with your audience.

In an Instant: Impromptu Speaking

Whenever you're speaking on the spot or with less than five minutes of preparation time, you're speaking impromptu. Impromptu speaking skills will help you in debates, because you'll have to clash with your opponents' arguments without being able to anticipate exactly what they're going to say. Also, this type of speaking is a great skill to have for asking and answering questions, either after a speech or as part of a debate. If you practice impromptu speaking, you'll be able to communicate dynamically on short notice, or even no notice at all.

TOOLS FOR TOP-NOTCH DELIVERY

Your voice is a powerful instrument for communication, and using it correctly takes significant skill and practice. A musician uses a variety of techniques to create quality sound, just as a speaker uses the voice to express ideas clearly and effectively. But there isn't a single 'right' speaking style. Although there are general strategies for successful delivery, you must develop your own style. Here are some of the basics when it comes to maximizing your vocal effectiveness:

> **Success Tip!**
>
> When a speaker captures your interest, think about why.

Rate. For the speaker, who's much more familiar with the speech than the audience members, the content may seem easily understandable when spoken at a pace that would be used for everyday conversation. However, when speaking in public, your rate must be slow enough so that your audience can clearly understand your ideas. Be sure, though, to keep your presentation fluent and lively. Although there's no rigid rule for the ideal speaking rate, most speeches are delivered at 120 to 140 words per minute. Also, you generally don't want to keep a constant rate throughout your speech. Slow down at your key points, or when the content is more difficult for others to understand.

> **Did You Know?**
>
> The world's fastest talker speaks at over 650 words per minute.

Pitch. Although there's no optimal pitch for public speaking, variety is very important nonetheless. It's rather boring for the audience if you maintain a constant and monotonous pitch throughout. Raise or lower your pitch to add variety and emphasis. This pitch variety should come naturally if you're comfortable with your speech and if you speak either impromptu or using an outline.

Pauses. In addition to helping you find your place or gather your thoughts, pauses can be used strategically. It's important to pause briefly after each of your key points or after you deliver vital information, so that the audience members have an opportunity to absorb the content. Also, pauses can be used to create dramatic impact after the most memorable and important lines.

Tone. It's important that your speaking tone reflects the intent of your speech. For example, a humorous speech should have a lighter, more upbeat tone; a tribute to fallen soldiers should have a more solemn tone; and a speech to persuade the audience to take some sort of political action should be delivered with a lively and passionate tone. In speeches intended to inform, even though the exact tone is less important in terms of reflecting the content, you should still be fairly lively in order to maintain audience interest.

Volume. Make sure that you're speaking loud enough so that the audience members who are farthest away from you can hear you clearly. You should watch carefully for reaction from the audience to determine if anyone is having difficulty hearing your speech. Very few speakers are too loud, but make sure you don't seem to be 'shouting' at the audience. Also, you don't necessarily have to speak at the same volume throughout. Some degree of volume variety is an effective way to deliver your speech in a lively, interesting manner.

Emphasis. In addition to pausing, your tone and volume variety can be used to emphasize key words and phrases in your speech. Any change in tone and volume can make a line stand out, such as raising your voice or deepening your tone.

Clarity. How you articulate words is critical if you want your audience to understand fully what you're saying. Make sure that you aren't mumbling or slurring your words, and practice any difficult words beforehand so that they aren't mispronounced when you speak.

THE SOUND OF SILENCE

On September 26, 1960, the debate between John F. Kennedy and Richard Nixon for President of the United States marked the first time that millions of people watched such a contest on television. The debate was rich in substance, with both participants conveying key insights into their respective platforms. Radio listeners were almost evenly split on who won the debate, leaning slightly in favor of Nixon. The story was very different with television viewers. They favored Kennedy by a wide margin. His youthful and upbeat image trumped the more tired-looking and pale Nixon.

Yes, body language does matter. You may think it shouldn't—that we should be judged only according to what we say. If so, Greek philosopher Aristotle was probably in your camp when he wrote in *Rhetoric*, "The battle should be fought on the facts of the case alone." Today, the fact is that people listen with their eyes as much as they listen with their ears. We usually think of audience members as 'listeners'. Perhaps it's a good idea to think of them as 'viewers' as well.

Excellent speakers communicate their confidence with their posture and movement. They don't rock back and forth or from side to side, instead placing their feet firmly on the floor. But that's only when they're in one place. Often, they move around the front of the room, adding color and emphasis to their points. Never ones to slouch, they stand with confidence—and that's what the audience sees in them.

Strong communicators add emphasis and style using gestures. To allow their hands to move freely, they keep them out of their pockets and off the stand. Although everyone has a different natural style when gesturing, here are some strategies to consider:

Avoid pointing your finger. Nobody likes having a finger pointed at them. For many audience members, doing so will appear too forceful. What if gesturing with your finger is a habit that you've formed and is a natural part of your style? At least be sure that you don't jab your finger directly at others, but that you point up, down, or to the side.

Limit closed-fisted gestures. The 'punching' gesture, like the finger-pointing gesture, appears a tad too blunt for many people. Some speakers see it as a way to show strength and conviction. Unfortunately, it also makes you seem more tense and rigid, in contrast to the more expressive and lively image you may want to present.

Do a '360' to expand your range. Most speakers restrict gestures to a very narrow range of motion. Their elbows stay right against their body, and their gestures are always in front of them or beside them. The best way to add variety to your gestures is to use the complete '360 degree' range of motion. In particular, you can emphasize your most important points with strong gestures above your shoulders.

Use a variety of gestures. We all have particular types of gestures that we use more often than others. They're part of our own natural style. Unfortunately, it can also become very repetitive and stale in the eyes of an audience member. If you have a chance to videotape yourself speaking, play your speech in fast-forward, and you'll notice this problem very quickly if it's the case with you. Do your best to use different gestures, so that your speech has more color and character.

Most importantly, be natural. Sounds contradictory, right? You've just heard several 'rules' for effective hand gestures, and now you're being told to be 'natural'. Undoubtedly, it's a tough balancing act. Your gestures are most expressive and effective when they come naturally, especially when your body is free of tension and stress. Try working within the framework of your natural style, but aim to enhance your performance on the dimensions mentioned previously.

Watch Out!	
Don't 'plan' hand gestures into your speech.	

DYNAMIC DEBATE DELIVERY

If you look at a debate score sheet, it's likely that no more than a quarter of the total marks are for delivery. Naturally, those who make excellent arguments but who are less comfortable with their delivery conclude that their speaking skills can't cost them any more than a fraction of the total score.

They're wrong. In an ideal world, this wouldn't be the case. We would judge debaters primarily by what they have to say. But each of us naturally makes subjective judgments. The impression you make as a speaker goes a long way in raising your score in all areas. People say to themselves, "That debater seems confident, and she really appears to have her head on her shoulders. So I guess her arguments are also quite strong, judging from how confidently she presents them."

In addition to the appearance of confidence, the range of speaking techniques discussed in this chapter applies to debate delivery. Several areas are particularly important:

Your use of variety and expressiveness. Even to the most interested listener, a debate can become dry if speech after speech is devoid of any passion. Make sure your style keeps the judges interested.

How clearly you present ideas. Judges have to grasp many distinct points, some of which may be rather sophisticated. It's important that you explain ideas very clearly and precisely, including good articulation and, if necessary, slowing down your pace.

The way that you write down your speech. A debate speech written out word for word makes judges feel like they're at a public speaking competition. Use an outline to show that you're confident enough in your ideas to be able to explain them without reading from text.

MASKING MISTAKES

Nobody speaks perfectly—not even seasoned professionals. We all make errors, as speech and debate is more of an art than an exact science. Unfortunately, we often let the audience know that we've made a mistake through our words, expression, or body language. Without doing so, most people wouldn't have even noticed! There are a few tools of the trade that make it easy to mask mistakes:

Don't apologize! Saying, "Oh, sorry, what I meant to say was ..." not only shows uncertainty, but it's also completely unnecessary. Why should you apologize, when you're the one making the effort to deliver a speech? Your credibility as a speaker depends on your ability to project confidence. Never give the audience a reason to believe that you're stumbling. Most of the time, your mistake will be so minor, that it has no significant impact on your overall message.

> **Success Tip!**
>
> Pretend that the error never even happened.

Pause. Sometimes, the most effective recovery tool that a speaker can use is not to speak. Too often, we fill memory lapses or mistakes with "um's" and "ah's," revealing that we've made an error. Why not just pause for a split second and collect your thoughts?

Recall what you just said. If you're struggling to find where you should be going next, use different language to summarize the thought that you've just finished. For example, you could say, "Now that I have established why physical fitness is enjoyable, I want to move on to ..." This technique not only gives you a moment to collect yourself, it also serves as a great transition to a new point.

Smile. A glum, flustered look is a blatant giveaway that you're struggling. If you're smiling and projecting a positive image, you'll be going a long way in hiding any mistakes.

THE ART OF ADAPTING

As a speaker, you're a 'servant' to the audience. Therefore, you must be flexible enough to adapt to the audience's reaction. The best speakers will pay careful attention to the non-verbal signals that audience members send to them and will adapt their speaking style or content accordingly. Here are a few situations with suggested responses:

> **Success Tip!**
>
> Notice the audience members' facial expressions.

Problem #1: Countering confusion. Say your listeners' facial expressions suggest that they don't clearly understand your point. They've stopped writing anything down, aiming to understand you first.

Solution: Engaging explanations. There's nothing worse than continuing as planned when your audience doesn't get what you just said. In this situation, you should repeat or summarize your point, explaining why it matters to the issue at hand. When you do so, maintain engaging eye contact with the audience members who appear uncertain. Also, moving forward slightly suggests that you're trying your best to help them understand what you're saying.

Problem #2: They're bored. Let's face it, not everyone will be interested in what you're saying. Some people will have a rather disinterested expression, others will sit back and cross their arms, and yet others will start looking down, to the side, or even at their watches!

Solution: Get dynamic! The main reason why they aren't interested is probably because *you* don't seem interested. Vary your pitch, tone, expression, speed, movement, and gestures to create some interest. Don't just keep your eye contact with those who are listening. To the contrary, aim to make eye contact particularly with those who seem bored. Make them feel like they *should* be listening.

Problem #3: Opposite opinion. Not everyone will agree with your points. Everyone, of course, has opinions, and sometimes you can tell that some audience members don't share your views. They may turn or shake their heads, or they may shift their posture. These signals reveal agitation or disagreement, and you must respond accordingly.

Solution: Decisive direction. You have two choices: defend your point assertively or focus primarily on other points. If you feel you have something more to say about your point that may convince the audience, don't stop with what you've planned. Be decisive in standing up for your argument, as those opposing you will either be convinced or at least acknowledge that you have sound basis for what you're saying. Another strategy is to play up other points and make them the main focus of your conclusion. In other words, if it seems like they don't agree with part of what you're saying, downplay these areas.

If you want to ensure that your speech content is delivered in an effective, high-impact way, be sure to practice the methods explained in this chapter. Great delivery leaves your audience with a favorable impression of both you and your speech.

Chapter 4: Keys to Success

✔ **Use an outline to deliver a speech.** Writing your speech down word for word makes it tough to have strong eye contact and engagement with the audience. Memorizing your speech makes your delivery seem unnatural, not to mention the extraordinary amount of time that you'll have to spend preparing. An outline with your key ideas provides helpful reminders as you go along, while allowing you to speak freely and naturally.

✔ **Practice effective speaking techniques.** A moderate pace with well-placed pauses makes it easy for the audience to follow your speech. Your expression, tone, and volume should reflect the purpose of the speech. Always make sure that your listeners can hear and understand what you're saying and that they get the desired meaning from the way you speak.

✔ **Enhance your speech with sound body language.** Your gestures help convey the tone and meaning of what you're trying to get across. In addition to making you *feel* more confident, a solid posture makes you *look* more confident. Remember that the audience members form much of their impression of you from what they see.

✔ **Don't make your mistakes obvious.** Apologizing shows weakness and uncertainty. Instead, pause briefly or refer back to what you've just said to help you recover.

✔ **Adapt constantly to your audience.** Pay attention to the body language and expression of the audience members to see if they're confused, bored, or in disagreement. Then, adjust your content and style accordingly. Your goal is to 'serve' your audience, and understanding your 'customers' is the first step to getting the job done right!

CHAPTER 5
Literally Speaking:
Speeches with Commentary

Coming Up!

Now that you've read what it takes to build a great speech, it's time to see the pieces come together. This chapter will take you through a few sample speeches, and the commentary will discuss what's going well and what could improve. Think about the style and tone you would use to deliver each speech.

SPACE TOURISM: REALISTIC OR RIDICULOUS?

Speech	Commentary

For most of us, the idea of a dream vacation that's 'out of this world' could include an adventure in Disneyland, a week on a Caribbean beach, or a Mediterranean cruise. But in 2001, millionaire Dennis Tito took 'out of this world' a bit more literally. He became the first person to take a vacation in space. Some people believe that space tourism is just another fad—a waste of time and money. I couldn't disagree more. Space tourism is the next frontier in our quest to explore the universe. Today, I'm going to tell you why space tourism is good for our dream to discover, the birth of a new industry, and a vision of human civilization in space.

Good personalization of the issue to open the speech.

Effective parallelism.

Blunt, clear opinion statement.

Human civilization has always dared to discover what we once thought would be impossible. Who would have dreamed of flying until the Wright brothers invented the airplane in the early 1900s? And who would have thought that a human being could walk on the moon before astronaut Neil Armstrong did just that in 1969? There's no question that past space missions have taught us a great deal about the universe, as well as creating more tangible benefits for science and technology. Space tourism is simply the next step in our dream to discover the world around us. It's time to encourage more people explore the universe, even if it's for no other reason than their own personal enjoyment.

A bit too abstract and general.

Good use of rhetorical questions.

Why would we care how these people spend their money?

So for those who have this dream, what will it take to get them there? Certainly, we could never expect governments to fund a person's desire for a very cool vacation. It's my view that the solution lies in the birth of a

Smooth transition.

space tourism industry, working in cooperation with the world's space agencies. If there
are wealthy people willing to spend hundreds
of thousands of dollars, if not millions of dollars, to make their space travel dreams a reality, why prevent them from doing so? Let's
allow investors and entrepreneurs to flourish
in their quest to take advantage of this opportunity. We've already heard that companies
like Virgin Airlines and Hilton International
want to be part of this dream. Space tourism
could be the birth of a new economic engine.

If we allow the dream to discover to come
together with the potential for profit, we'll
have completed the first step toward human
civilization in space. We'll have laid the foundation for permanent establishments that will
allow more and more people to take a holiday
on, say, the moon, or perhaps a space hotel
orbiting our planet. Surely, this vision may be
decades away, but a space tourism industry
is the first stage in making it come true. It
will plant seeds of opportunity that will inspire a mission reaching far beyond just a few
wealthy individuals.

My friends, we must always dare to
dream, and we must always dream to discover. We must explore this new frontier made
possible by advanced, modern technology.
And we must embark on a mission to take
tourism 'out of this world'.

*"Working in coopera-
tion" how exactly?*

*How do they want
to be "part of this
dream?"*

*Did you explain how
they would "come
together?"*

*Making sweeping
generalizations.*

*Good link back to the
first point.*

*Effective flow from
"dare [to] dream [to]
discover."*

*Good connection to
opening of speech.*

COMMENTARY ON "SPACE TOURISM" SPEECH

This was a fairly creative speech likely meant for a light, informal occasion. The goal was to present a viewpoint on a concept rather than on specific ideas.

What did the speech do well?

• *Use of vivid language.* It was clear that establishing an emotional connection with the audience was one of the speaker's main goals. The use of rich, descriptive language helped in this regard. Phrases like "dare to dream" and "birth of a new economic engine" illustrated some of the key ideas.

• *Closing linked to opening.* The "out of this world" expression used twice in the introduction was repeated in the conclusion. "Dream to discover" and "frontier" were also used again. The use of similar themes and phrases, as well as a personal connection, made for a good fit between the introduction and the conclusion.

• *Use of rhetorical questions.* Especially in the second paragraph, rhetorical questions encouraged the audience members to imagine the concepts for themselves. This aided the speaker in achieving his goal, which was to make an emotional connection.

• *Transitions between points.* The first sentence of the second and third paragraphs included a clear reference to the previous point. This allowed the speech to flow smoothly and helped the speaker guide the listener along a particular path.

What could have improved?

• *Length of introduction compared to body paragraphs.* Normally, an introduction of this length would be appropriate. But in this case, it was the same length, if not longer, than each of the main points. A shorter introduction or longer body paragraphs would have made the proportions more suitable.

• *Too abstract and general.* Granted, making an emotional connection was an important goal of this speech. However, more concrete, factual information and details would have been useful. The speech came across as 'dreamy' more than practical or realistic.

• *Extends the case too far.* The main thrust of the speech was clearly space *tourism.* Discussing space *civilization* as well appeared rather fanciful and unfocused.

MERCK, MECTIZAN, AND RIVER BLINDNESS

Speech

Commentary

Unbearable itching. Skin disfigurement. Permanent blindness.

Effective imagery.

Welcome to the world of one of the 18 million people in the poorest of countries who suffer from river blindness. Welcome, also, to one of the most daunting dilemmas faced by a corporation in modern times. Today, I want to tell you about the story of an American pharmaceutical firm mandated by its shareholders to maximize profits, but motivated by its heart to help humanity. I want to tell you about the story of Merck, its drug *Mectizan,* and the millions of people who needed it but couldn't afford to pay for it. To start, I will explore Merck's dilemma in the 1980s. Then, I will tell you about what they did. And finally, I will discuss what this means for the future of drug development and distribution.

Good use of parallelism here.

Overview of theme.

Is this an advertisement for Merck?

"Tell them what you're going to tell them" introduction.

Merck faced a tough dilemma in the 1980s, having to decide whether to spend millions of dollars on a drug that would never earn a dime. The disease was river blindness, known scientifically as "Onchocerciasis." I'll spare you the pronunciation and call it "river blindness" from here on in. Spread by an infected blackfly's bite, it results in a parasitic worm infesting the body. The intense itching, skin disfigurement, and permanent blindness that would occur affected millions of people.

Clear statement of the key point.

Wasn't it called "river blindness" already?

Reinforcement of imagery.

Merck, though, had stumbled upon research that could cure this terrible disease. The problem was that nobody was willing to pay for it. There was little commitment from governments, and the end users certainly weren't in any position to afford it. To make matters worse, there was no distribution system, as the people afflicted by river blindness lived primarily in isolated rural areas throughout many African countries. Should Merck spend millions of dollars to develop its drug *Mectizan*? If so, should it give it away for free? And if it gives it away for free, should it take care of distributing the drug? And if it did all of these things, would it set a dangerous precedent for future drug development? Merck faced all of these daunting challenges, and it was a 'go' or 'no go' decision. There was no halfway solution. They would either go full steam ahead, or abandon the project.

So how did Merck resolve this dilemma? Simply put, it decided that it would do away with profits and sink millions of dollars into solving this problem, even though it knew the company would never recover more than a fraction of its investment. In 1987, Merck announced that it would give away *Mectizan* for free to all those who were afflicted by river blindness. Merck's campaign, particularly the Merck *Mectizan* Donation Program, eventually engaged many other groups. These included pharmaceutical companies, governments, non-profit organizations, and the World Bank. In 1994, the World Bank approved a special program to raise $130 million toward treating river blindness in developing countries. Millions of doses later, the lives of so many had been changed for the better. What started as an uncertain venture by one company turned into

Statement of the overall challenge.

Good use of questions to describe the dilemma.

Three questions is okay, four pushes it.

Repetition of the same point three times, perhaps too many.

Good link back to first point of the speech.

A clear description of what actually ended up happening.

How many doses exactly?

a global operation engaging partners and affected communities alike.

No detail of "affected communities" link.

The case of Merck's success raises interesting issues for the future of drug development and distribution to those who can't afford to pay for medicine. Today, this issue comes up repeatedly in the mission to treat HIV/AIDS throughout the developing world, because the drugs are too expensive for most people to afford. It's my view that the model developed by Merck is a useful one for other health programs. The key is that the burden not be placed squarely on the shoulders of one company. Merck took the risk that it wouldn't have significant support, but the support eventually came. Other drug companies need to be assured that they'll have willing partners to shoulder part of the responsibility should they want to engage in such a humanitarian effort. I certainly hope that this problem can be solved. Surely, *Mectizan* did set a precedent. But I would argue that it was a good precedent to set.

"Interesting?" Use a different word.

Why it's relevant today.

Who specifically should carry the burden? Governments? Other companies?

Good opinion statement.

Nice lead into the conclusion.

Today, I've shared with you Merck's dilemma, what it did to resolve this dilemma in favor of human health, and what this means for future medical endeavors in developing countries. In 1987, a group of people decided that unbearable itching, skin disfigurement, and permanent blindness didn't have to be a reality. The world didn't have to accept that nothing could be done about it. Something was done about it, and it sent a ray of hope to millions of people around the world.

Once again, reinforcement of opening imagery.

Isn't the main point what it means for the future?

COMMENTARY ON "MERCK AND MECTIZAN" SPEECH

Although the speaker spent two points describing what happened in the past, the purpose was clearly to show that what Merck did should be a model for present and future situations. It was both a speech to inform and a speech to persuade, with the informative parts laying the foundation for the persuasive remarks.

What did the speech do well?

• *Use of imagery*. It was important for the audience to picture the effects of river blindness. The opening phrase, "Unbearable itching. Skin disfigurement. Permanent blindness," was one instance where imagery was used effectively.

• *Insight into the primary actor*. The speaker was effective at explaining Merck's dilemma, discussing its conflicting objectives and specific challenges concerning *Mectizan*. This allowed an audience member to think, "What would I do if I had to make that decision?"

• *Providing relevance to the issue*. Without describing the future implications of Merck's endeavor, many audience members would have been left asking, "So what? It's all fine and well to *know* about this dilemma, but why does it *matter?*" The discussion of related situations provided present-day context to the speech.

• *Relevant factual information*. The speaker gave the audience members key facts about the disease, the dilemma, and the solution to help them understand the situation. If more facts had been stated, it would have been harder for the listeners to grasp the most important ones.

What could have improved?

• *Less promotion of Merck*. There's no question that the speaker intended to paint Merck in a positive light for its role in this situation. At times, though, the tone seemed overly gushing in its praise of Merck, almost making it seem like the speaker was trying to impress someone who worked at the company.

• *Different focus in the conclusion.* If a key objective of the speech was to explain to the listeners how Merck's model should apply to present and future disease outbreaks, the conclusion shouldn't have focused so much on what happened in the past. Saying, for example, "Let's extend this ray of hope to millions more," could have been one line of a more effective closing.

• *More discussion of the present-day solution.* Granted, it wouldn't be wise to overburden the audience with too much factual information. That being said, it would have been helpful to characterize in more depth what a model for solving current situations would look like.

Chapter 5: Keys to Success

✔ **Notice the importance of having a clear objective.** You could be forgiven for wondering what the key goal was in the "Space Tourism" speech, as the speech seemed to lack focus. The "Merck and Mectizan" speech did a more effective job of moving toward a relevant, important, and practical message.

✔ **Pay attention to the type of language.** The "Space Tourism" speech used vivid, colorful language in order to make an emotional connection. The "Merck and Mectizan" speech combined richly descriptive and factual language, reflecting both the human dimension of the situation and the practical aspect of the dilemma, respectively.

DISCOVER DEBATE:
HOW TO WIN AN ARGUMENT

Part III

CHAPTER 6

Nuts and Bolts:
Building Blocks of Debate

Coming Up!

Now that you've seen what it takes to make a great speech, it's time to discover how to debate. This chapter will tell you about the nature and process of a debate. You'll learn how to define resolutions, play your role, use a flow sheet, and work with your partner. Rounding out the chapter are tips to enhance your performance in a number of areas.

DIVING INTO DEBATE

Simply stated, a debate is a clash of opposing views, thought to lie somewhere in between a formal discussion and a formal argument. (Most debaters will tell you that it's far closer to an argument.) Although panel debates may involve a number of different perspectives, almost all competitive debates focus on a specific topic. This topic is known as a resolution or proposition. There are two sides in a competitive debate: the *Affirmative* and the *Negative*.

> **Did You Know?**
>
> The world's longest debate lasted for 503 hours and 45 minutes.

The Affirmative side argues in favor of the debate's resolution. It goes first in the debate, allowing it to set the tone for the round. The team supporting the resolution may also be known as the Proposition or, in parliamentary debate, as the Government.

The Negative side speaks against the resolution, placing it in direct opposition to the Affirmative. It must respond according to how the Affirmative has defined the terms of the resolution and set out its case. In parliamentary debate, the team opposing the resolution is known as the Opposition.

An odd number of judges, most commonly three, decides the winning team. In most styles of debate, the panel members vote independently for the team they feel won the debate. Sometimes, though, the judges have a discussion following the debate—a 'debate on the debate'—in an effort to arrive at a consensus decision.

BUILD IT UP, BURN IT DOWN

Debate can sometimes seem daunting and complex. With so many people flaunting their mastery of big words, technical terms, weighty-sounding phrases, and intricate arguments, it's no wonder that many students find debate confusing. In reality, it's much simpler than that. Great debating really boils down to two simple objectives:

1. **Build a case with strong arguments and supporting details**. Develop a series of points that are compelling enough to convince your judges and tough enough to withstand criticism from your opponents. Support your points with sound explanations and evidence. Arguments

are planned before the debate begins, except for the Negative team in an impromptu debate. They are the core ideas that form a case. Each team will typically make between four and six constructive points, which are also known as contentions.

2. **Counter the other team's arguments with refutation**. Tell your judges in plain language why your opponent's points are wrong. Demonstrate that the other team hasn't built a case strong enough to prove its side of the debate. Refutation, which is also called clash, is vital to any debate. It involves the point by point opposition of the other team's points. While well-developed constructive arguments and evidence are necessary for a solid case, the debate round is often won or lost in the refutation.

THE ARRAY OF RESOLUTIONS

Debate resolutions come in a variety of forms. The same topic may be stated in different ways, and the distinctions may seem trivial. But the way it's stated can change the dynamics of the debate. Before looking at the types of resolutions, let's look at the two ways to write them:

A debate topic may be written as a question. For example, "Should the Government consider driving while talking on a cell phone to be impaired driving?" or "Should assisted suicide be allowed?" In each case, the Affirmative is answering "yes" and the Negative is answering "no" to the question.

A resolution may be stated as a phrase. In this form, a debate resolution usually begins with a standard phrase, such as "Resolved:" or "Be it resolved that," and it continues with a statement. For example, "Be it resolved that a national identity card should be implemented" or "Resolved: entrepreneurs and bankers are more essential to society than artists and writers."

True vs. False: Propositions of Fact

Propositions of Fact are debates over the truth or reality of a statement, often of a historical or technical nature. Since they tend to be fairly academic, they aren't commonly used for competitive debating. Not all Propositions of Fact involve answers that are definitely true or definitely false. You may come across a 'true vs. false' resolution of a speculative nature. Of course, this makes it tough to decide which team won the debate. Here are a few examples of this kind of topic:

- Resolved: The world is not prepared for a global flu pandemic.
- Resolved: Debt payments are the primary cause of African poverty.
- Resolved: Privatizing the water system would save money.

Good vs. Bad: Propositions of Value

Propositions of Value are debated on grounds of morality or worth. They don't involve a plan, focusing instead on the strengths of an idea or principle. The values up for debate may concern moral, social, economic, political, or cultural issues. Debates on values resolutions are the most subjective, because they involve an argument on competing beliefs, not on issues of absolute truth or the feasibility of a plan. Here are some examples of Propositions of Value:

- Be it resolved that children do not have a right to privacy.
- Be it resolved that international sport has a place in politics.
- Be it resolved that multilateralism is preferable to unilateralism.
- Be it resolved that following orders is no excuse for war crimes.

Change vs. No Change: Propositions of Policy

Policy resolutions involve a debate over whether a system needs to change and, if so, whether the plan proposed is effective and workable. The Affirmative team must establish both of these elements to prove its case. The Negative team will attack the needs as invalid and the plan as unworkable. In rare cases, the Negative team will propose a counter plan, whereby it agrees with the needs for change but proposes a significantly different and more effective plan to solve the problem. Here are some examples of Propositions of Policy:

- This House would develop a mandatory recycling program.
- This House would create an agency to censor the Internet.
- This House would strengthen regulations on genetics.
- This House would implement a mandatory vaccination system.

DEFINING THE DEBATE

The first responsibility of the Affirmative team is to define the terms of the resolution. This process should take no longer than 20 to 30 seconds and should provide a clear framework for the debate. Many students define every word, which is almost always unnecessary.

For example, if the resolution is "Be it resolved that television has a negative influence on teenagers," here's a possible definition: "We define 'television' as the television entertainment media, and we define 'negative influence' as encouraging harmful behavior in society." Notice that "teenagers" was left undefined. The term implies a certain age group, and the exact age isn't central to the debate.

The Affirmative team does have a certain degree of flexibility in how it defines the resolution, and the Negative team must debate on these grounds. If you're the Negative team, don't challenge the definition unless absolutely necessary. Contesting the definition lowers the quality of the debate and the impression you make on the judges. Even so, the Affirmative's definitions must be reasonable.

For example, if the resolution is "Be it resolved that the United Nations should be judged a failure," here's an example of a fair definition: "The Affirmative defines 'the United Nations' as the UN Security Council and 'judged a failure' as not meeting its founding goal of maintaining international peace and security." Notice that the Affirmative left out other functions of the United

> **Watch Out!**
>
> Don't protest a definition simply because it was unexpected.

Nations, such as humanitarian relief. This is fair, because the Security Council is a central part of the United Nations and provides sufficient basis for debate. The Negative team shouldn't bring up humanitarian aid as part of the case, unless it can relate its arguments directly to the issue of international peace and security.

A debate comes down to who, on balance, presented a stronger case. Since the debate is subjective, neither of the teams can prove its case definitively. A debate is 'shades of grey' rather than 'black and white'. In the above example, it would be impossible to say that the United Nations Security Council is a complete success or a complete failure. The reality lies somewhere in between, and it's up to the debaters to argue which perspective is more correct.

FOR A TRUE DEBATE, AVOID TRUISMS

A resolution is not allowed to be defined such that it's literally impossible to debate. For example, if the resolution is "Be it resolved that women are better than men," the Affirmative can't define "better" as "the ability to have children." If it did, the Negative wouldn't have a fair opportunity to present a case. A definition of this nature is called a truism and is grounds for the Affirmative to lose the round. You're not allowed to make the resolution true by definition, since doing so makes the contest one-sided.

Reasonable (and smart) debaters will always avoid truisms. Unfortunately, either unintentionally or as an ill-advised trick, your opponent may present one. How do you respond if the Affirmative brings up a truism? The best approach is to spend no more than 20 to 30 seconds explaining why it's impossible to debate within the prescribed definition. After challenging the definition, find an aspect of the case closely related to the resolution that can be debated.

In the case discussed above, you could make the debate about whether women are more effective at raising children. Although you should technically win the round on the unfair definition alone, there's no use having an entire debate about definitions. A 'definitional debate' will leave a bad impression with the judges and almost certainly lower your speaking scores as well, even if they agree with your interpretation of the resolution.

SET THE SCENE: TIME-PLACE-SET CASES

Usually, a debate takes place in the present on a circumstance that's actually happening. Is a particular practice good or bad? Do we need to change the present system? All of the important facts are known to the debaters, and they can all be used to build cases. However, some of most exciting debates take place on matters of history or on real or fictional scenarios. Enter the time-place-set case, where you get to set the scene of the debate.

Point in History

In this type of time-place-set debate, the Affirmative has to say *when* the debate is taking place, *what* the decision is, and *where* it's occurring. Once the Affirmative has defined the terms on these dimensions, neither side can bring in any information that would not have been known at the specific time and place. So, even if everyone knows the eventual result, the debate takes place assuming that this isn't the case. It's common to ask the Chairperson to assume the role of the person making the decision. Here are two examples:

• **Ronald Reagan at the Berlin Wall**: "Mr. Chairperson, you are Ronald Reagan, President of the United States of America. The date is June 12th, 1987. You're about to deliver a speech on the Western side of the Berlin Wall. Tell the Soviet Union to tear down this wall."

• **Merck and River Blindness**: "The year is 1987, and you're the head of Merck, one of the world's largest pharmaceutical companies. You've developed a drug called *Mectizan*, which helps treat and cure the river blindness disease that has impacted hundreds of thousands of people in many countries, primarily in Africa. They can't afford to pay for the drug. Give it away for free."

Scenario

Great debates can take place on scenarios that actually happened, were seen in a movie or television show, or are completely made up. In this type of case, the debate is about the principles involved in the scene. It's especially important that the Affirmative is very clear in presenting all of the facts in the case, because any cause for confusion will make it tough for a good debate to take place. Here are some examples of scenarios used as time-place-set cases:

• **Hockey Suspension**: "You're the head of the disciplinary committee for the National Hockey League. One of the players injured a player with his stick, in retaliation for an earlier hit. Normally, this offence would result in a suspension for at least three games. However, this player is known as one of the most ethical players in the league—a true role model. He has apologized, and you consider this to be an isolated incident. Make an exception, and don't suspend him."

• **Car Accident Lawsuit**: "Madame Chairperson, your child was injured by a careless driver while she was riding her bike. She will eventually make a full recovery. You can sue the careless driver and are very confident that you'll be awarded compensation, which you believe you rightly deserve. However, the careless driver is a single mother with two sons, and the judgment would force her to the verge of bankruptcy. Don't sue her."

THE DEFINITION OF 'CROSSING THE LINE'

We've already discussed truisms, which are prohibited because they're technically impossible for the Negative team to debate. But what about definitions that are technically debatable, but unfair nonetheless? You may be thinking to yourself, "Virtually everything is debatable, so how can any definition of the resolution possibly be

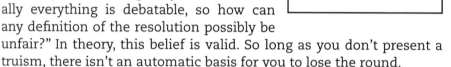

Watch Out!

Don't try to win debates by using clever definitions.

unfair?" In theory, this belief is valid. So long as you don't present a truism, there isn't an automatic basis for you to lose the round.

What about in practice? Debates are judged by people who expect you to be reasonable. More specifically, this means that you can't define the topic in such a way that another debater can't reasonably be expected to argue against it. Ask yourself this question: "If I was facing another team who did what I am planning to do, would I consider it to be fair?" If you answered "no," then your judges would probably think it's unfair as well. The numerous instances of unfair definitions, all of which should be avoided, are discussed below:

Morally reprehensible opposition. It's expected that debaters will have to defend positions that they don't agree with or that are controversial. There is a limit, however, to how far you can go. You aren't allowed to define a topic in such a way that it calls for a Negative case so morally reprehensible that virtually nobody in society would agree with the position. For example, you can't expect the Negative team to defend racism, slavery, murder, or terrorism.

Specific knowledge. According to the guidelines of most debate tournaments, your definition must be such that an informed, well-educated person would be able to debate it. Specific knowledge cases arise when you define a resolution so that the debate to follow requires technical expertise on the subject. For example, you can't expect the Negative team to have detailed knowledge about molecular biology, a little-known court case, or an isolated historical event.

However, you can bring up cases that could conceivably be made complicated, so long as you stick to principle-based arguments that everyone can understand. Take a debate on the use of in vitro fertilization for human reproduction. If you defined the resolution and introduced the case in a way that allowed for a debate on competing principles, it would be acceptable. If, however, you brought up highly technical and scientific issues, it would be considered unfair. (It could be fair if you know that your opponents learned about it in biology class and that your judge is a science expert.)

Violates the resolution's intent. The two points above relate primarily to impromptu resolutions. This point focuses on debates on resolutions that are explicitly stated. In these types of debates, the Negative should have a reasonable opportunity to prepare a case, even if it has to adapt it to a reasonable, but unexpected, Affirmative definition. If you're the Affirmative, you aren't allowed to present a definition that clearly violates the intent of the resolution.

Say the topic is, "Resolved: the USA should tone down its international rhetoric." It's widely accepted that the debate is about the United States of America. It would be unfair to define "USA" as the "Underwater Scientists Association" (if one actually exists, that is). No reasonable person could have expected such a definition, so it would reflect very poorly on your team.

THE ARCHITECTURE OF A DEBATE

While there's no universal standard for the structure of a debate, most rounds follow a similar basic framework. The first part of a debate round consists of constructive speeches. During this phase, debaters from both teams have an opportunity to present new arguments, to defend their team's previous points against attack, and to criticize

> **Did You Know?**
>
> The earliest political debates took place in Athens.

their opponent's arguments. The second part of a debate is the rebuttal phase. This segment is each team's opportunity to analyze the debate as a whole and to make a final pitch for why it has won the argument. On the following page is a simple structure for student debating:

1st Affirmative Constructive (1AC):	7 minutes
1st Negative Constructive (1NC):	7 minutes
2nd Affirmative Constructive (2AC):	7 minutes
2nd Negative Constructive (2NC):	7 minutes
1st Negative Rebuttal (1NR):	4 minutes
1st Affirmative Rebuttal (1AR):	4 minutes

Of course, the format of debate varies depending on where you're debating and at what level. Although the general skills are relatively similar, you'll have to adapt to the specific circumstances. This standard format is often called academic style debate. Although the limitations of a single book make it impossible to explore in detail the intricacies of each style, here are a few areas in which you may see a departure from the academic debate format outlined previously:

Did You Know?

Bill Clinton, Oprah Winfrey, and Brad Pitt were once debaters.

Speakers per team. Usually, there are two debaters representing each team. But in some styles, each side is represented by a single debater who plays both constructive and rebuttal roles. Other times, you'll see three debaters per team, with one member per team focusing exclusively on the rebuttal speech.

Questions and answers. The discussion style of debate features a question and answer period up to 10 minutes long between the end of the constructive section and the beginning of the rebuttal section. Debaters go back and forth asking questions to the other side and answering questions posed by their opponents. This style is often seen at younger age levels.

A more difficult type of question and answer format is the cross-examination style. After each of the four constructive speeches, a member of the opposing team has three to four minutes to question the speaker, hoping to draw out admissions or to expose flaws. Cross-examination debate is discussed in Chapter 10.

Parliamentary style debate, discussed in Chapter 9, is yet another format involving questions and answers. The difference compared to discussion and cross-examination styles is that the questioning doesn't take place in a defined period. Rather, Points of Information are questions asked as interjections by a seated debater during an opponent's constructive speech.

Breaks. You may encounter a style in which there is a three to five minute break before the rebuttal part of the debate. This gives each team an opportunity to discuss and plan its rebuttal strategy.

Number of rebuttals. A single rebuttal speech for each team is the norm in most cases. Some styles, though, allow both members of the team to present a rebuttal. In total, there would then be four rebuttals. Such circumstances usually involve shorter rebuttal speeches. The partners have to work together to divide rebuttal responsibilities effectively.

Order of rebuttal. Similar to how the prosecution usually goes last in a court trial, the Affirmative normally delivers the final rebuttal speech. Some styles switch it up, allowing the Negative team to have the last say. This changes the dynamics of the rebuttal, giving the Negative a slight advantage over the Affirmative.

Time per speech. The amount of time allotted to each speaker varies significantly between different debate styles and formats. Constructive speeches are rarely less than five minutes long or more than 10 minutes long. Rebuttal speeches are generally between three and five minutes in length. In total, the time for the whole debate is usually between 35 and 50 minutes.

PLAY YOUR ROLE

Each speaker in the debate has different responsibilities. Although how well you debate will have a large impact on your performance, it's also important to be debating well in the right areas. It's essential that you understand the role you have to play in your speech. These roles vary between debate styles. Using the basic debate format outlined previously, the following pages discuss each speaker's responsibilities. The diagram on the next page summarizes these functions.

1st Affirmative Constructive (1AC)

The first speaker's role is the most straightforward, yet it's critically important to the debate. Your speech sets the tone for the round and

Speaker Roles in a Debate

1st Affirmative Constructive
1. Define the resolution
2. Introduce the case
3. Present arguments

1st Negative Constructive
1. Introduce the case
2. Present arguments
3. Clash with the Affirmative

2nd Affirmative Constructive
1. Present new arguments
2. Clash with the Negative
3. Defend past arguments

2nd Negative Constructive
1. Present new arguments
2. Clash with the Affirmative
3. Defend past arguments

1st Negative Rebuttal
1. Refute the Affirmative
2. Contrast competing themes
3. Summarize the Negative

1st Affirmative Rebuttal
1. Refute the Negative
2. Contrast competing themes
3. Summarize the Affirmative

lays out the key issues. There are three functions that the first Affirmative speaker should perform:

1. **Define the resolution**. Spend roughly 20 to 30 seconds making it crystal clear what the debate is about. Without first presenting a definition, none of your arguments or any of your opponent's arguments will have a well-described context.

2. **Introduce the Affirmative's case**. Presenting your core themes isn't a requirement, but it's highly recommended. Like the definition, a brief description of what you plan to accomplish helps set the tone for the debate. Make it clear what your themes will be and what, in a general sense, the judges can expect from you. Some debaters opt to state what their partner's focus will be. This presents a clearer picture to your judges, but be careful not to steal your partner's thunder.

3. **Present constructive arguments**. Once you've told the judges where you're going with your case, at least two and not more than four constructive arguments are necessary. These points will form the majority of your speech. Be sure to develop each of your arguments completely. Without a strong set of initial arguments, the first Negative speaker will be able to tear down your case and present a strong Negative case before you've been able to construct a solid case.

1st Negative Constructive (1NC)

The first Affirmative speaker will have set the tone in a way that favors its side of the resolution. At this point, the ball is in the Affirmative's court. Your challenge is to level the playing field or, hopefully, to gain the advantage. In figurative terms, you're trying to tear down their fortress and build up your own. Here are the recommended responsibilities of the first Negative speaker:

1. **If necessary, contest the Affirmative's definitions**. The words, "if necessary" should be taken seriously. Should the first Affirmative speaker present grossly unreasonable definitions, you can only challenge them at the beginning of this speech. After that, it's too late—you've forfeited the right to stake your claim. If you decide to contest them, do so quickly and move on.

2. **Introduce the Negative's themes**. Claim your ground. Tell your judges exactly where you plan to go with your case, namely what your themes will be. Similar to how the Affirmative has described what it sees as the main issues, you should try to seize the agenda and explain what you believe are the core issues and why. Although you don't have to perform this role, doing so will be invaluable in helping you go head to head with the Affirmative, which has the advantage of setting the agenda from the outset.

3. **Present constructive arguments**. Technically, you usually don't have to make constructive arguments if you're the Negative team. While you could stick to refutation, your case will be much stronger if you build a set of strong constructive points. Depending on the time limits and how much time you want to spend on refutation, you'll probably only be able to present two, or at the most three, main arguments.

4. **Clash with the first Affirmative's arguments**. This role is absolutely central to your speech. Without it, you'll leave the impression that you've conceded the Affirmative's key arguments. Spend time on point by point refutation of the first Affirmative speaker's arguments. Generally, you want to spend approximately half of your speech on clash, either before or after your constructive arguments.

2nd Affirmative Constructive (2AC)

The definitions have been settled, the main themes have been laid out, and the initial arguments have been presented. Now the debate gets messy. The second constructive speeches are when the grueling process of jockeying for position takes place. The first speakers have hit the tee shots, and now it's your job to play the fairways in order to setup a strong finish. Here are some of the areas that the second Affirmative speaker should cover:

1. **Develop new constructive arguments**. There's no way that your team can present a thorough and effective case in your first speech alone. You should aim to build two or three more arguments for your side, which will help strengthen your case. Make sure that your arguments are distinct from your partner's points. To stake out your place in the debate, center your arguments around a distinct theme.

2. **Clash with the first Negative's points**. No second Affirmative speech is complete without a comprehensive, point by point clash of the first Negative speaker's arguments. Even though the burden falls on you to prove your case, Negative arguments to the contrary must be proven inadequate, irrelevant, or incorrect.

3. **Defend the first Affirmative's points**. After the first Negative has clashed with your partner's points, there are two ways to build them up again. The first way is to reinforce them with further details and explanation. While this can be helpful, it may also suggest that your partner wasn't thorough. The second and usually advantageous method is to 'clash with clash', explaining why the first Negative speaker's refutation was wrong. This approach follows the logical flow of debate more closely than adding supporting material.

2nd Negative Constructive (2NC)

The second Negative speech is the final opportunity to bring new constructive matter into the debate—the closer of the 'meaty' part of the round. Unfortunately, it can seem even tougher than the second Affirmative speech, since there are so many previous arguments to analyze and discuss. Your main task in this speech is to setup your team for a powerful rebuttal. Here are the key roles for this pivotal position in the debate:

1. **Present new constructive points**. Remember, the only significant opportunity for your opponents to clash with your new points is in the rebuttal. Since they would rather be spending their rebuttal time summarizing the debate, a number of solid arguments in this speech can really throw them off.

2. **Challenge the second Affirmative's points**. Clash with the Affirmative's final constructive arguments so that the rebuttal is free for you to bring the debate down to core themes.

3. **Defend your partner's points**. Using similar techniques as the second Affirmative speaker, reinforce the first Negative speaker's points. Explain why the second Negative speaker's refutation didn't actually defeat your arguments.

If a debate is supposed to be a continuous back and forth flow, haven't we left something out? What about challenging the second Affirmative speaker's defense of the first Affirmative speaker's points? This would essentially be 'clash of clash of clash', and if it sounds confusing, it's because it is. That's why it's best to avoid doing this in your speech. Adding a fourth objective would leave you little time for each one, likely making your analysis rather shallow.

1st Negative Rebuttal (1NR)

The rebuttal speeches are very distinct from the constructive speeches. So far, we've had a back and forth flow of arguments and refutation. By this point in the debate, all of the main points have been laid out, and most of the lines of attack have been explored. Think of the Negative rebuttal as a closing argument in a court trial. It's your final 'sales pitch' for why the resolution should be defeated. Although the format of a rebuttal speech is the most flexible, here are some of the Negative rebuttal speaker's responsibilities:

1. **Provide an overall refutation of the Affirmative's case**. Notice the word "overall." That is, it shouldn't be a continuation of the point by point clash heard earlier. Your goal is to highlight key aspects of your refutation, explaining why the Affirmative's general themes are incorrect or haven't been proven.

2. **Compare and contrast key themes**. Provide your interpretation of the Affirmative's themes and how they relate to your themes. In essence, you're saying, "We talked about this, and they talked about that. Here's why our themes were superior." Especially in a complex and confusing debate, this tactic can clarify the round for your judges and make their decision easier. They're usually appreciative—and rewarding—when a rebuttal speaker clarifies the round for them.

3. **Present a final summary of your case**. Remind the judges of your case and its key points. Yes, you've presented the points, summarized them at the end of each speech, and heard them refuted in your opponent's speeches. Isn't that enough? Probably not. Make absolutely certain that your judges know exactly what pillars your case stands on, particularly the overall case themes.

1st Affirmative Rebuttal (1AR)

The objectives of the Affirmative's rebuttal speech are similar to those of the Negative's rebuttal speech. It's a closing argument—the final word in the debate. Use your 'closer' position to your advantage by saying frankly and convincingly what the debate is about, and why you won. These are the key roles of the Affirmative's rebuttal:

1. **If necessary, refute the second Negative's new points**. The Negative rebuttal speaker faces a paradox. A rebuttal is supposed to focus primarily on general themes, and only secondarily on specific arguments. On the other hand, you don't want to leave your opponent's new points uncontested. If you can wrap your clash into your overall refutation, it's best to do so. However, you may want to clash briefly with the second Negative speaker's new arguments. Should you decide to take this route, focus on the key elements only.

2. **Refute the Negative's case as a whole**. Like the Negative's rebuttal, you need to explain clearly and persuasively why your opponent's case is wrong. If you've clashed with the Negative's new constructive points in the opening of your rebuttal, make sure that this part of your speech is a clear departure from point by point clash.

3. **Draw a contrast between the two sides**. Interpret the themes and areas of contention the way you see them. If the Negative rebuttal speaker has done something similar, be sure to explain why your analysis of the key issues is more correct. That is, make it clear why your issues should be the deciding issues of the debate.

4. **Summarize your case**. You may be constrained by time at this point, so it's best to plan a short and to the point summary. Reinforce the key reasons why the judges should support the resolution. Remember, the burden generally falls on you to prove your case, so your core arguments must stand strong at the end of the debate.

GET INTO THE GAME: FLOOR SPEECHES

Were you itching to be part of that memorable final round, but the decisions didn't quite go your way? Despair not, for you have a golden opportunity—at least *after* the official debate is over. In most tournaments, there are 'speeches from the floor' at the end of a final round. While the judges have left the room to make their decision, it's the audience's turn to have the final say.

A floor speech is short, usually 60 to 90 seconds long. You can support the Government, support the Opposition, or speak for 'cross-benches'. The last option means that you don't want to backup either side, but that you want to provide compliments, criticisms, or commentary on both sides of the debate. (Perhaps you don't want to give either of the teams any credit, since *of course* you would done far better had you been in the round.)

GO WITH THE FLOW (SHEET)

Debates get very lively and dynamic, with multiple arguments and counter-arguments made by each speaker. Judges are often left confused, without a clear picture of where the debate is going. Equally important, debaters may find it difficult to plan their line of attack without an organized 'picture' to help them understand the debate. A flow sheet that keeps track of the back and forth flow of the debate is one of your most important tools in forming your strategy. How specifically will a flow sheet be useful to you?

Planning your clash. Writing down your opponent's points in a clear and organized manner makes it far easier and quicker for you to figure out how to respond. You'll be able to make sure that you've covered all of the key parts of your opponent's case.

Defending your points. Noting how your opponent has clashed with your arguments lets you know what you need to come back to and defend. Especially if your opponent's clash was disorganized, a flow sheet makes it clear which of your points were attacked and weakened and which ones have been left undamaged.

Checking for consistency. Another use of the flow sheet is to check the logic and consistency of the arguments. By laying out your opponent's case in an ordered, point by point way, you can determine more easily whether there are gaps in logic or contradictions between the points. Likewise, you can make certain that your arguments and counter-arguments do not contradict each other and that they flow in a clear and logical way.

Preparing the rebuttal. Planning an effective rebuttal requires you to have a clear sense of the debate as a whole. A flow sheet gives you a snapshot—a 'road map' of sorts—of how the constructive part of the debate played out. This allows you to identify what your team should focus on in the rebuttal speech.

Taking notes for your speech. You don't want to be turning and reading scores of pages when you take the floor. A quick glance at your flow sheet tells you exactly where you are and where you need to go.

Hopefully, you're now convinced that a flow sheet will be useful to you in multiple ways. So, how do you go about making one?

Step #1: Divide your page into columns. The most basic system involves dividing the page into two columns, one for the Affirmative team and the other for the Negative team. This helps you keep your page neat and tidy. Unfortunately, this method makes it tough to see how the arguments and counter-arguments are flowing from speech to speech. You may find it more useful to divide your page into one column for each speaker—First Affirmative, First Negative, and so on. If you employ this approach, consider using a sheet of paper that's larger than the standard size.

Watch Out!

Avoid writing down minor details on your flow sheet.

Step #2: Write down and number each point. As a member of the opposing team makes points, write them down in the order they're presented. It's absolutely essential that you number the points, even if your opponent didn't do so. Otherwise, you'll lose track as the debate goes on. Under each point, you could have a few supporting details if you feel they're an important part of you counter-attack. Don't forget to write down your points as well so that you can keep track of your opponent's refutation.

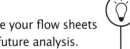

Success Tip!

Store your flow sheets for future analysis.

Step #3: Draw arrows in order to gauge the flow. As a debater refutes one of the other team's arguments, whether it's your partner or your opponent, draw an arrow from each point to the correspond-ing clash. This will help you determine quickly which points have been refuted and, if necessary, whether you need to provide further defense of your previous arguments.

WINNING WITH A DYNAMIC DUO

You may be thinking, "Oh great, here comes the section about mushy, gushy teamwork stuff." Well, these "mushy, gushy" concepts are often what make or break a debate team. Debate is a team sport. Your team's success won't depend only on the individual strengths of both debat-ers. It will also depend in large part on how well you and your partner work together. Why is a strong team central to success in debate?

You look unified in front of judges. Although judges have to assign speaker scores to each individual, much of their evaluation is based on their overall impression of the team's performance. They want to see you and your partner operating in a unified, complementary way. What they don't want to see is two people battling each other for the spotlight. And they'll also be far more impressed if your debating styles appear compatible.

Your speeches reinforce each other. A debate isn't a set of independent speeches. Your team's speeches are part of an overall case approach. They must flow naturally and complement one another. When a team works well together, debaters are more likely to defend and refer back to a partner's points.

You can adapt on the go more easily. You'll never know exactly what the other team will say in its speeches. While your opponent has the floor, whispering or passing notes can help both of you find a strategy to deal with its arguments. In many cases, you won't know how to clash with a particular argument, but your partner will have a tip to pass on to you.

Debate becomes much more enjoyable. Both before and during a tournament, you'll probably spend many hours with your partner. There's nothing worse than having a team whose members don't get along, but merely tolerate each other for the sake of debate. Debate is also a social activity, so the friendship between you and your partner is important. If you're enjoying the experience, it will reflect positively in your speaking style. You'll likely be less tense when you speak, and you'll seem more lively and dynamic.

MAKING A SMART SELECTION

Now that you know why effective teamwork is important in debating, the next step is to think about how to select a partner. This will be one of the most important decisions you make in debate. Unfortunately, it can also get very personal and political. (Debaters, for the most part, are naturally competitive people.) Here are some tips to keep in mind when selecting a partner:

Try to find someone who is at a similar level. There's no sense in having a team with one very seasoned debater and another who's just starting out. The stronger debater will feel that his or her partner is dragging the team down. The less experienced member will feel like an underperformer. What's worse is that the team will appear unbalanced in the eyes of the judges. Partnerships work best when both members learn from each other and progress together.

> **Success Tip!**
>
> Use practice rounds to see if a debate partnership will work.

Don't select a partner purely on personal friendship. Granted, being friends with your partner is important for some of the reasons described previously, such as working well together. But a word of caution: a strong friendship doesn't always make for a solid debate team. Be certain that you can justify your selection to yourself on dimensions other than the person being your best friend.

Aim for complementary styles. Two debaters with very similar styles—both very aggressive, or both very passive—can pose challenges. The judges may form unfavorable generalizations, such as 'too hostile' or 'too shy'. At the same time, you don't want to be polar opposites with your partner. It probably isn't the greatest idea to have an extremely aggressive debater paired with a very shy debater. The team simply won't look coherent. The trick is to strike the right balance. For example, one debater may be slightly more analytical, the other slightly more passionate.

Consider commitment level to debate. It's not uncommon for debaters to be involved in many extracurricular and leadership activities. Make sure that your schedules mesh, both for preparation and tournaments. If you're someone who considers debate your top priority but your partner wouldn't hesitate to miss a tournament for a dance practice, think twice about the prospect of debating together.

WORKING TO WIN

You have a great partner. You're ready to work together. Both of you are committed to doing whatever it takes to improve and win. Now is when the real work begins. What are some of the tips to remember when debating together?

What gets said between partners, stays between partners. There's nothing wrong with discussing a debate issue with many people. In fact, brainstorming with a larger group is a great idea. But don't give away your game plan. It can be tempting for friends to discuss their respective strategies before a tournament. You would be surprised at how quickly word gets around. Many debaters are mystified when they hear one of their very unique and key arguments used against them by an opposing team.

Work interdependently on the case. Some teams prefer to prepare a case independently. They decide who's playing each speaker role and assign complete responsibility for the speech to that individual. This makes as much sense as a hockey team's forwards training together and its defensemen training together, without the two groups ever working alongside each other to form a common strategy. Speeches have to fit together. While final preparation for a speech outline can be left to each debater, it's best to form a case jointly. Both partners need to have a sound grasp of all of the team's points, and that's most likely to happen if the team works on the case interdependently.

Bounce ideas off each other. Have one partner propose an idea, while the other member argues against it. This approach will accomplish two goals. Firstly, you'll be able to test the strength of the argument and see if it can withstand criticism. Secondly, if you find that the point is strong enough, you'll at least have anticipated some likely points of refutation against the argument.

Evaluate your performance constructively. Effective teams learn from their mistakes and build on their strengths. Talk to your partner after each round and at the end of a tournament to identify how *both* of you can improve in the future.

Share credit and blame equally. Crediting a win to the supposedly 'stronger' debater or blaming a loss on the allegedly 'weaker' debater is a sure way to damage the team's future performance. You compete as a team, you win as a team, and you lose as a team. Period.

LESS COULD BE MORE: PREPARING TO DEBATE

Conventional wisdom is that the more you prepare for a debate, the stronger you perform. Isn't it common sense that the top debaters are the ones who spend many weekends and late nights preparing scripts for every speech and every possible argument? Not necessarily.

Of course, this doesn't mean that you don't have to worry about preparation at all. What it means is that you have to prepare the *right* information, not everything that may come up. The level of preparation necessary will depend on how experienced you are and on your personal preferences. Below are discussions of pre-debate strategies for prepared and impromptu debates.

Prepared Debates: Get a Grip, But Not Too Tight

If you know the resolution far in advance of the tournament, you should be very comfortable debating it beforehand. This means understanding the issue well enough that you can mold and adapt your team's case to each debate. But it doesn't mean spending a dozen hours writing down text for every possible circumstance that could come up. Here are some tips to follow:

Watch Out!

Don't read points from prepared text.

Avoid fully prepared speeches. If anything, only your first Affirmative speech should be fully prepared. After that, you shouldn't have word for word speeches ready to go. Why not? It's a debating tournament, not a public speaking tournament. If you've written out your speech, it will be obvious to your judges that you've done so. They'll be asking themselves, "Is this person debating, or just reading out a prepared speech?" More importantly, you won't be focused on responding to the specifics of what's happening in the debate.

What if you're just starting out and only feel comfortable with prepared text? Firstly, you may need to step out of your comfort zone and experiment with a less rigid structure. Secondly, if you absolutely need to have something ready, keep it to a minimum level. Perhaps you can prepare some text for part of your new constructive arguments. But write out no more than that.

Have ready a few more arguments than you need. If you're the Negative team, you'll want to have ready more than your primary, preferred case. Why? The Affirmative's definition and case may lead you in another direction. This doesn't mean having every point prepared in extreme detail. But write a sentence or two to describe a handful of points other than your key ideas. Even if you're the Affirmative team, your second speaker may need to use different arguments if the Negative team takes an unexpected approach to its case.

Think of some possible ways to clash. The key word here is, "think." That means not preparing detailed, scripted refutation for dozens of possible arguments. Surely, you should have an idea of how you would go about responding to numerous opposing arguments. And it's probably helpful to jot down a few notes. However, there should be much more thinking than writing taking place.

Impromptu Debates: It's All in the Name

They're called 'impromptu' debates for a reason: your planning should be held to a minimum. You'll receive the topic roughly 15 minutes in advance. Any preparation should be limited to the following:

Affirmative cases. Most impromptu tournaments feature at least some open-ended resolutions (see Appendix A for examples), which means you can define them however you want. It's a good idea to come into a tournament with at least half a dozen cases ready. You don't need to be as prepared as you would for a tournament in which the topic has been announced well in advance. The extent of preparation should be general knowledge about the issue and a set of points to form the

Affirmative case. If you come into the round too prepared, your judges won't be too impressed by your lack of *impromptu* debating.

Negative processes. Since there are thousands of possible debate issues, you can't possibly prepare to go up against even a fraction of them. You'll definitely get to know about many issues as you debate more often and stay on top of current affairs. Preparing arguments for and against different possible resolutions may be good practice. But you should focus your thinking on processes. How will you work as a team to react quickly to the Affirmative's case? Who will speak in each position? What general format could you use to present your case? This won't take much time, and it shouldn't. Go into the round comfortable in knowing how you'll work together, but be ready to adapt your style to what the Affirmative team presents.

> **Did You Know?**
>
> The Negative team wins most impromptu debate rounds.

THE "KISS" PRINCIPLE

"Keep It Sweet and Simple!"

Many debaters believe that complex arguments and big words will help them win. They may make you look smart, but that doesn't always translate into effective persuasion. Your case is as good as it's understood by the judges. You don't score any bonus points for complicating it. Here are some ways to simplify the debate:

Use 'us vs. them' distinctions. By stating pairs of opposites, you can actually use your opponent's case to make your case more clear. "Prevention vs. bandage solution," "innovation vs. old ways," and "decisive action vs. complacency" are examples of such pairs. This tool helps the judges understand what exactly you're trying to get across. It can also paint your opponent's case in a negative light. If you're arguing against giving prisoners the right to vote, you could summarize an argument by saying, "This point affirms that criminals must be temporarily removed from society, whereas the Affirmative would rather let criminals participate actively in society's democratic system."

Include analogies, metaphors, and examples. Sometimes the most effective way to help people understand a complex idea is to compare it to something simple. For example, "Just like Churchill wanted to take the battle to the enemy's turf during the Second World War ..." or "Our case is akin to fixing the hole in the ship so that we don't have to continue bailing out the water." But be careful when using these tools. You don't want to trivialize the debate and appear to be making sweeping generalizations. Also, you want to make sure that your judges can identify with your comparison. Bringing up an actress whose name your judges have never heard before or a scientific discovery that isn't well known may be more confusing than clarifying.

Use clear, direct language. If your quest is to demonstrate your mastery of the English language and all of its intricacies, you may end up losing your judges. Suppose you want to talk about the "fundamental fallacy inherent in the philosophical premise of the Negative's second constructive argument." Try this instead: "The Negative's second point is false because ..." It's good to use intelligent language, but don't make what you say needlessly and excessively complicated.

Avoid unknown acronyms and 'inside' language. We often think that if we know a particular acronym or commonly used jargon, so will everyone else. If you're talking about the "U.S.," the "E.U.," or another widely known acronym, it won't be a problem. But don't assume everyone knows that "O.A.S." stands for "Organization of American States" or that "T.R.C." stands for "Truth and Reconciliation Commission."

WATCH THE CLOCK

Wouldn't it be nice if we could simply go on and on until we've finished what we have to say? Unfortunately, this would make debates drag for longer than the audience would like. Debaters have to comply with strict time controls. There's nothing worse than being in the middle of your final constructive point when the timekeeper cuts you off. Budgeting your time carefully will improve your performance.

At each minute, the timekeeper will signal to you how much time you have left. There will also be time signals when you have 30 seconds left, when your time has expired, and when your grace period—usually 15 seconds—has finished. At the end of this grace period, you must sit down. No exceptions!

How do you pace yourself accordingly? To start, you must know if you're on track to finish on time. (Usually, debaters have a great deal to say, so finishing early is less of a problem.) Say you're the first Negative speaker, and you have to clash with three Affirmative points and present three of your own. If you have seven minutes to speak, it's a good idea to allow approximately 15 seconds for your introduction, 45 seconds for your conclusion, three minutes for clash, and three minutes to present arguments. Generally, this 'minute per point' rule for both refutation and construction serves as a useful guide. A signal that you have two minutes left when you've just finished your clash and are starting your first constructive argument is a sign that you're behind. This would leave you roughly half a minute for each argument, which isn't enough time for thorough development.

What if you can tell you're behind? Firstly, catch up sooner rather than later. You'll find it much easier to adjust when you have more time to work with. By the time you have only one or two minutes left, your task becomes far more challenging. Secondly, you can use one or more of the following strategies to make sure you finish on time:

Cut out an argument. If you have at least three arguments and one of them isn't pivotal to your case, you could decide to eliminate it. Of course, this leaves your case weaker, but it can be more effective than merely skimming over a greater number of arguments.

Condense each argument. As mentioned previously, it's important not to skim over arguments just to get them in. However, if you can cut out nonessential, embellishing details, you can still be fairly thorough while making sure that you complete each point.

Sacrifice some refutation. You could either refute each of your opponent's points more quickly or not clash with one or more points at all. The first tactic is usually superior, because it's important that you challenge every important point made by your opponent. In most cases, though, shrinking the refutation slightly is preferable to sacrificing constructive matter that's critical to your case.

Go light on the conclusion. Undoubtedly, tying up your speech and providing reminders to your judges are useful functions of your conclusion. But they're also not critical to the case itself. If you only have to cut out a few seconds from your speech, keep your conclusion to a sentence or two so that you don't have to leave out valuable constructive or refutation matter.

THE INTRICACIES OF ETIQUETTE

Being respectful and polite won't score you any extra points with your judges. Rather, it's a basic expectation. On the other hand, failure to follow proper debate etiquette can leave a bad impression and cost you dearly. The rules of etiquette are simple, but important. Here are some of the basics:

Before the Debate

• *Acknowledge the judges when you enter the room (or when they enter).* Make eye contact and smile, but don't shake hands. Doing so seems tacky, as if you're *trying* to impress them.

• *Wish your opponents "good luck" or shake hands.* As with the judges, it's a good idea to acknowledge the other side in a respectful manner. Even though you're about to go head to head with them, you want to show that you're being a good sport.

• *Avoid pre-debate chit-chat.* Write your names, your speaker positions, and your team code on the board, and then take your seat. Even if you're friends with the debaters on the team opposite, don't start making conversation with them about the previous round or last night's party in front of the judges.

During the Debate

• *Don't talk to your partner too loudly.* If you need to communicate, do so in writing or by whispering very quietly. Talking audibly while your opponent is speaking appears rude and distracting.

• *Avoid rude body language.* You'll hear many things that you disagree with, or that you consider to be plain wrong. It's usually best to keep your reaction to yourself. Sometimes, subtle body language can be appropriate, such as a slight shake of the head or a puzzled look. But sighing loudly or throwing up your hands in disagreement are some of the reactions that appear inappropriate.

• *Address your opponents respectfully.* As much as possible, address your opponents by title, such as "the first Affirmative speaker" or "the Leader of the Opposition." Saying "those guys" or "the speaker over there" seems overly informal, if not impolite. Also, when you're attacking your opponent's points, don't make it personal. Avoid phrases such as, "I can't emphasize enough how ridiculous Jim's first argument sounded." Using language like "Here's what's wrong with the Negative's first point" is the best approach.

After the Debate

• *Avoid profound reactions to the judges' decision or comments.* In many tournaments, the winning team is announced immediately after the round is finished. Whether this is the case, or even if the judges are only providing constructive comments, don't show any boastful celebration or grudging disapproval. Be respectful both to your judges and to your opponents.

• *Shake hands with your opponents and the judges.* It's poor taste to dash hastily out of the room. Be sure to thank the judges for their time and to congratulate your opponents for a good debate.

• *Stay respectful in the hallways and central meeting areas.* Just because a debate round is over, it isn't a license to criticize your opponents or judges. Competitive debating is usually a tight-knit community, and word does get around. Worse yet, you may be overheard. You could end up with the same judges in the future, and you could face your opponents once again. Perhaps one day you'll even end up as partners with one of them.

WORKING THE ROOM

As discussed in Chapter 4, your visual impression is a vital part of how effective you are at communicating. In debate, where you stand and how you use movement will have an impact on your performance. You'll often be constrained by the setup of the room, so it's important to know how to adapt to a variety of arrangements. On the following page, you'll see an example of how a debate room may be setup, as well as the 'power positions' for stance and movement.

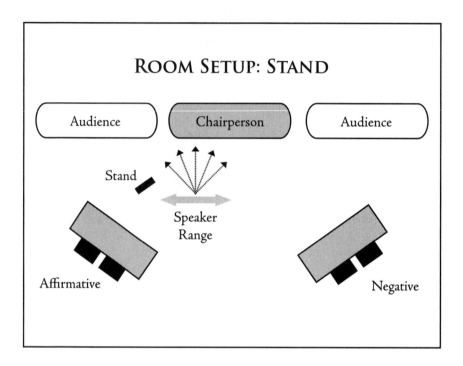

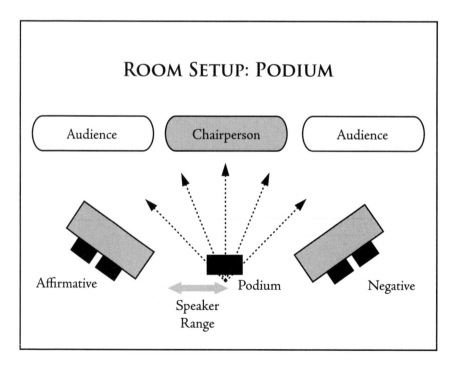

Taking a Stand

Where you stand—your physical placement—makes a difference to your delivery. Judges 'listen' not only with their ears, but also with their eyes. When you have the floor, you want everyone's attention to focus on you. Here are some tips to improve your stage presence:

Step out from behind the table. Although some debaters prefer standing behind the table, this approach doesn't allow you to show commanding stage presence. In order to be most effective, you need to be in front of the other debaters so that you stand out from the group.

Capture the middle. Our eyes naturally focus on the center of the room. Standing in the middle also brings you closest to the most number of judges. Of course, you don't want to veer onto your opponent's side, so it's usually best to place yourself slightly off center toward your side of the room.

Not too close, not too far. Standing too far back weakens your stage presence. It almost makes you seem shy, and it becomes tougher for you to project your voice to the entire audience. But standing too close to the audience isn't the best of ideas either. Judges like their personal space, and placing yourself too close to them makes you seem overly infringing and forceful. Be sure to strike a good balance.

Don't 'hide' behind the stand. You can definitely use your stand to place your notes, but it should never be used as a 'clutch' for your hands. If you're constantly grabbing and fidgeting with the stand, chances are that you'll become stiff and appear to be talking into your stand more than to your audience.

Prancing Around the Podium

Podiums and stands are necessary evils. You need them to place your notes, but they present a physical barrier between you and the audience. This leaves many debaters wondering if they should even bother using one. Unfortunately, the alternatives are usually less desirable:

Avoid placing the papers on a desk or table. Although this method may seem preferable to the obstruction of a podium, the problem with it is that you have to look too far down to see your papers. When you refer to your notes, your posture will be weakened because you'll have to lean over slightly, and your eye contact will also suffer.

Try not to have cue cards in your hands. This often used and mis-used method is rather tempting. After all, it eliminates the movement restriction imposed by a stand. Unfortunately, it can be very distracting when a speaker gestures with cue cards in his or her hands. If you're wedded to this option, use small size cards. If not, you're better off keeping your hands free to gesture more expressively.

How do you go about using a stand? One of the most effective methods is to place a diagonally-slanted stand a few feet toward the side of the room. This allows you to stand in the center, with nothing in front of you acting as an obstruction. The stand will still be visible to you, but it will not get in the way. Also, this method makes it far less tempting to grab and lean on the stand.

A podium is generally immovable, as it's placed firmly in the centre of the room. In this case, it's usually best to use it. Make sure that you stand slightly back from the podium so that you can move and gesture freely without being tempted to lean over or hold onto it.

DRESS FOR DEBATE SUCCESS

This comment isn't intended to tell you how to be the most fashionable person in the room. (There are plenty of magazines devoted to the subject.) Rather, it's meant to give you a few tips on how to dress appropriately for a debate tournament. Your dress is an important part of the impression you give to your judges. Dressing either too informally or too elaborately takes away from your performance.

Ladies should be careful not to seem too fancy. Sure, bright pink may work if you're trying to stand out at your graduation. But it's probably too bold for debate. Any combination that looks neat, simple, and professional will work well.

Gents look best with a suit and tie, especially for a championship tournament. If you prefer to dress down a bit, lose the jacket or the tie. But avoid wearing khakis, jeans, or anything that will make you seem too informal. Make sure you wear dress shoes. (Even if you agree that debate is a sport, runners won't do the part.)

DON'T PROP YOURSELF UP

The use of visual aids is usually welcome in public speaking. Speakers use flip charts, refer to the board to explain their points, or hold objects in their hands to help illustrate an idea.

However, props aren't welcome in a debate. Firstly, they look tacky. Your ability to persuade and explain should rest solely in the power of your voice and physical expression. Secondly, most debate styles consider it against the rules to use props. An astute judge will deduct points if you use them. In short, avoid props like the plague.

STAND UP COMEDY: HUMOR IN DEBATE

The use of humor is ripe with rewards but fraught with pitfalls. You'll either strike a home run by making your judges laugh or strike out by leaving everyone wondering why you're trying to be funny. It's fairly tough to learn how to be funny, as it has to come naturally from within you. Here are some general tips to keep the joke from being on you:

Don't force humor into your speech. Humor isn't necessary. You won't lose any points if you aren't funny. Too many debaters think to themselves, "I've noticed debaters who are funny and how much judges seem to like them. So, perhaps I should try to do the same thing." It won't work.

> **Watch Out!**
>
> If you're not sure that your joke is funny, don't say it.

Keep the jokes clean. Most judges won't be receptive to inappropriate or offensive humor. A crude remark will stand out in your judges' minds—for the wrong reason.

Make sure the humor applies to the debate. Your humor will be more warmly accepted if it illustrates an idea that's part of the round. A witty analogy, for instance, can be a very useful refutation tool. Isolated jokes meant purely for the sake of being funny won't help you much.

The information in this chapter, particularly defining the resolution and playing your role, should serve as a foundation for you as we move into the sections on making arguments and counter-arguments.

Chapter 6: Keys to Success

✔ **The first objective in a debate is to prove that you're right**. You accomplish this goal by developing constructive arguments. When the other side clashes with your constructive arguments, your task is to defend them.

✔ **The second objective in a debate is to prove that the other team is wrong**. You accomplish this goal through refutation of its arguments. Specifically, your task is to clash with every relevant point made by your opponent and to explain why its overall case is incorrect.

✔ **Start the debate round with a clear and fair definition**. Definitions should be used to focus the debate on a particular area or to clarify ambiguous terms. Avoid unfair definitions that leave the Negative team with limited room to debate. As the Negative side, only contest a definition in the rarest of cases.

✔ **Play your role in the debate**. It's important to know when you should be constructing your team's case and when you should be refuting the other team's case. Also be aware of the ways in which a rebuttal speaker has different responsibilities than a constructive speaker.

✔ **Use a flow sheet to keep track of arguments**. Write down, in columns, the arguments and counter-arguments made by each speaker. Then, use this visualization of the debate to plan your team's strategy and to help you when it's your turn to speak.

✔ **Practice sound teamwork skills**. Think very carefully about whom you want as a partner, as strong teamwork and well-matched styles are important. Treat debate competition as a team exercise that requires you to work with your partner.

✔ **"Keep it Sweet and Simple!"** Following the "KISS" principle will increase your effectiveness as a debater. Avoid unnecessary complexity, so that it's easier for your judges to grasp the points that you're trying to communicate.

✔ **Practice good etiquette**. Whether before, during, or after a debate, it's essential that you're respectful to your competitors and to your judges.

✔ **Stand where you can be most engaging**. If the room setup allows, capture the center, give yourself enough room to move around, and don't let the stand be a barrier.

CHAPTER 7

Pros and Cons: Solid Points and Powerful Cases

Coming Up!

The heart of top-notch debate is a great case by both teams. In this section, you'll learn how to engineer strong, intelligent arguments centered around compelling themes. You'll also see how to present your points in a way that leaves your judges impressed and your rivals facing an uphill battle.

BUILDING A CASE FROM THE GROUND UP

The foundation of a first-rate performance is a strong case. A case is a collection of individual arguments that push for or against the resolution. Your team is responsible for presenting a case that articulates your side of the issue clearly and effectively. What are the ingredients of a case that's tough enough to withstand attack?

Consistent. The arguments you present must fit well with one another. The need for consistency applies both within your speech and between you and your partner. Without this coherency, your case will be easy to refute and hard to defend.

If the arguments are *independent*—each one, standing alone, helps build your case—they must never be contradictory. Say that your partner argues, "Economic globalization is good because of the benefits associated with greater international trade." Then, you stand up and present the argument, "Information globalization is good because the spread of knowledge allows countries to produce more locally, making them less dependent on foreign imports." These two independent arguments are inconsistent.

If, however, the arguments are *interdependent*—they're linked and support each other—the relationship must make sense. For example, if you talk about the "shortage of doctors in developing countries" and proceed to call for "sending more medical equipment to solve this problem," you have a consistency problem. What good is more medical equipment if there aren't enough doctors to use the equipment?

Explained. It isn't enough simply to state strong, focused points. You have to explain completely *why* they're correct. Say you're the Affirmative team and you're debating on the resolution, "Be it resolved that the entertainment media has a negative influence." One of your arguments is, "Many children commit violent acts because of what they see on television." Don't stop there. Why is television the cause? How severe is the problem? Is the problem widespread, or are we talking about a small number of shows? Do the harmful shows overshadow the positive ones? Always leave your audience with a complete sense of what each argument means.

Supported. If your explanation isn't enough to make an argument convincing, you may need to draw on evidence to support your claim.

Say that in arguing post-secondary education should be free, you talk about how "many people can't access it because they don't have enough money." Really? How many people are you referring to? What proof do you have that making it free for everyone is even necessary, when the government could simply increase grants and loans? As discussed in Chapter 3, be sure to use credible sources and strong examples.

Organized. How you lay out your case is extremely important. Don't just randomly state argument after argument. Think about how to split the arguments *between* speeches and how to organize them *within* a speech. A well-organized case is easy to follow, which also makes it easier to secure the agreement of your judges.

There are many different ways to organize your points, and the method you should select depends on the resolution. Refer back to Chapter 3 for a discussion of the more common structures. One possible way is to start with the need and then to describe the solution. For example, you could start by explaining why environmental pollution is a growing problem, and you could continue by presenting a number of initiatives. Or, perhaps it makes sense to organize your case by themes. For example, you could talk about the security reasons for engaging in a war, and your partner could talk about the human rights reasons. While there's no 'right' way to organize a debate case, think carefully about how to make it logical and easy to follow.

Complete. Make sure that you cover the key angles of an issue to the extent that the definition requires. If you're arguing that the government should subsidize community league sports, you could argue that the primary reason is to improve health and wellness. But what about the positive impact on the community? While you could make a great case on the healthy lifestyle issue alone, your case would be stronger if you covered several key advantages. However, a word of caution: don't cover every angle at the expense of depth. Make sure that you have enough time to cover every key area of your case with sufficient logic and sound explanations.

Relevant. Seems common sense, right? You would be surprised at how often intelligent people make intelligent arguments that don't get to the heart of the issue. Say you're arguing that Supreme Court judges should be elected. One of your points could be that the court is deeply divided on several key issues and that a shakeup of the system is in order. But would electing the judges actually change that? Is it even relevant to the competing principles that are at the core of the debate? Make sure that all of your points support your case directly.

THE RIGHT ANGLES: ANALYZING THE ISSUE

We'll soon get into the specific types of arguments that you can use to support your case. First, it's important to understand how to go about analyzing an issue. While there's no 'one size fits all' framework for this endeavor, there are five key areas to look at when learning about a topic: *Political, Economic, Social, Cultural,* and *Moral.*

Political. Think about issues in terms of how they play out in the public arena. What are the implications for diplomatic or security relations between states? What does the state of the national political dynamic mean for society?

Economic. This angle of analysis deals with material well-being. Some of the relevant issues include trade, unemployment, standard of living, taxes, investment, and subsidies.

Social. Examine the impact of the issue on relations between people in society. Specifically, what are the main implications for families, schools, workplaces, and communities?

Cultural. This area of analysis relates to a society's sense of identity and character. Some of the key areas include the arts, media, languages, and multiculturalism.

Moral. An analysis of the issue's moral dimensions involves 'right vs. wrong' questions. For example, is it ethical to lie about a medical condition in order to prevent fear? Or would it be morally acceptable for a doctor to remove a dying patient's life support system?

A THEME TO SET THE SCENE

Debates with scattered, disorderly arguments lack a sense of direction. Granted, the definition should do a fairly good job of making the scope of the debate clear. But you need to go a step further in order to

to spank their children, you could argue, "Allowing spanking provides a sense of legitimacy to other forms of violence that could also be used to discipline young children."

Morality. Issues of morality consider whether a practice is 'right' or 'wrong' from a values perspective. Since such judgments are personal in nature, making an argument on moral grounds can be challenging. But appealing successfully to a common belief and explaining why it's a worthwhile value may strengthen your case. On the issue of foreign aid, you could argue, "Increasing our monetary commitment to international development is the right thing to do, because it advances our society's concept of universal human dignity."

Consistency. If a practice related to the issue has been firmly established, you can argue that that your view is a justified extension of this circumstance. Say you're arguing that American citizens born abroad should be allowed to run for President. You could argue, "Our democratic system trusts foreign-born Americans with important, high-responsibility positions, such as Governor of California, and sensitive national security roles, such as Secretary of State. Allowing them to run for President would be consistent with these principles."

Remedies. If an injustice has occurred in the past, you can argue that the victims are justified in demanding compensation or another remedy. For example, you could say, "Reserving a set number of places in medical schools for students of aboriginal ancestry is justified, because aboriginal peoples were denied a fair opportunity in the past."

Rights. You can justify a principle on the grounds that it's a fundamental right or freedom. The crux of such an argument is that the right at stake is too important to be taken away simply because of a particular circumstance. It's helpful to explain why limiting the freedom is harmful. In a debate on restricting hate speech, you could say, "The right to speak freely is undeniable, even if it's used in a way that's morally objectionable. We shouldn't be trying to draw an arbitrary 'line in the sand' when it comes to this cornerstone principle of a free society."

Norms. Your point can appeal to one's sense of what's considered normal or commonplace. But don't forget that a norm to one person may not be a norm to another. Only use this tool if virtually everyone in society accepts the norm that you're thinking of evoking. For example, you could claim, "This practice infringes on the parent-child bond, which is the most fundamental relationship in our society."

Historical. Citing historical reasons can help you justify either upholding or rejecting a current practice. Using history as an argument to maintain a current practice can be risky, as it begs the reaction, "That was in the *past*. This debate is about what's justified in the *present*." More often, a team will argue that a historical reason is no longer sufficient justification. For example, you could argue, "Many of the historical reasons for protecting a citizen's unrestricted right to bear arms don't exist today. We now have well-established police forces to protect everyone in society, so it's no longer appropriate for citizens to take the law into their own hands."

Precedent. You can argue that a certain practice sets a precedent for future actions. Although sometimes there is a positive precedent, a dangerous, 'slippery slope' precedent is the type most often cited in debates. For example, one could argue, "Censoring school library books sets a dangerous precedent for academic and literary freedom. The logic used to justify censoring library books can also be used to justify censoring newspapers, textbooks, and other information sources readily available within the walls of a school."

Arguments on Systems

Enforceability. It's all fine and well that a system is brilliant in theory. But if it can't be enforced fairly and effectively, you can make an argument relating to this problem. Say the debate is on whether there should be a law against parents smoking at home in the presence of their children. You could argue, "The sheer difficulty of enforcing such a law makes it unworkable and weak."

Effectiveness. Even if a system has worthy goals, it may not be effective at meeting its goals. You can argue for or against a system based on how well it carries out its stated mandate. Say you're making the case for trade sanctions against a dictatorship that's abusing the human rights of its citizens. One of your arguments could be, "Diplomatic sanctions and United Nations resolutions have proven ineffective, so we need to take a harder line." On the other hand, your opponent could argue, "Imposing trade sanctions wouldn't be an effective solution, because it wouldn't weaken the grip of the country's leadership on the military and police forces."

Feasibility. A proposal is worthy of praise only to the extent that it's practical to implement. You can make an argument supporting or opposing a system on the basis of its feasibility. If you're debating the issue of Internet regulation, you could say, "The problem with trying to form a global Internet 'watchdog' is that its excessive costs and bureaucratic hurdles would overshadow any potential benefits."

Abuses. Even if a system has worthy goals and is easy to operate, you can argue against it on the grounds that it's prone to abuses. Take a debate on the right of prisoners to communicate privately with the outside world. A possible argument is, "Granting this right leaves the door open to abuses, such as prisoners conducting criminal activities through unfettered communication with their associates."

Results. One of the most common ways to judge a system is to evaluate its outcomes, either positive or negative. These benefits or harms can relate to one or more of a variety of groups, such as families, communities, companies, countries, or the world. For example, you could argue, "As a result of insufficient environmental regulations on factories, the unacceptably high level of urban smog pollution is negatively impacting human health."

Arguments on Perception

Image. You can make an argument relating to the reputation of a person or group. To strengthen this type of point, explain *why* having a good image actually matters. In a debate on school discipline policy, one could argue, "A zero-tolerance policy would improve the reputation of the city's public schools in the eyes of parents. This would lead to greater trust and a more cooperative relationship between parents and school administrators."

Signals. An argument can be based on the signal that an activity or circumstance sends to other people. It's helpful to take this type of point a step further, explaining *how* the signal has either a positive or a negative impact on society. An example of this technique is, "Allowing prisoners to vote in national elections sends the message that they're a full part of our democratic system, which would lead many people to question the integrity of the electoral system."

Attitudes. A policy or situation can impact how people *think* about an issue, and what people think can impact what they *do*. Say the debate is on the merits of graduated, multi-stage driver licensing. One side could argue, "Adding steps to the process would help dispel the care-free attitude that many teenagers have toward driving. It would cause more young people to recognize that driving is a dangerous activity requiring responsible behavior."

Culture. An argument on culture is similar to one on attitudes, except that it deals with the overall *mood* rather than what a segment of the population *thinks* about an issue. For example, you could say, "Modern magazines paint a harmful stereotype of the 'perfect' body image. This creates an unfavorable culture in which teenagers are judged by their peers according to this standard."

Arguments on Behavior

Influence. You can argue that a circumstance has a positive or negative impact on human actions. The goal here is to establish a cause and effect link. One could argue, "The television entertainment media has a negative influence on children because much of its programming encourages violence in schoolyards and neighborhoods."

Intent. A point can be based on the intent of a person or group as it behaves in a certain way. This intent may either be positive or negative. It's important to explain the link between *intent* and *result*. For example, you could make the point, "Tobacco manufacturers intended to target a young audience so that they could establish an early base of loyal consumers. This ended up increasing the percent of teenagers who smoked cigarettes."

Role. Points based on role consider *who* is carrying out an action. You can argue that the person or group playing the role should or shouldn't be doing so. If looking at an individual's role, one could make the point, "It's the role of parents, not teachers, to encourage students to eat healthy foods." If analyzing a role from a non-personal standpoint, you could argue, "Acting as a 'global police force' and stopping humanitarian crises is a necessary role for the United States of America, which is the world's only superpower."

WEAK AND WOBBLY ARGUMENTS

Each argument should be a clear, direct reason for the judges to agree with your side. Unfortunately, many debaters use inappropriate tools to build a case, meriting a discussion of the most common pitfalls:

Claiming that public opinion is on your side. A debate isn't about whether a view is *popular* or *unpopular*. It's about whether a view is *right* or *wrong*. Of course, a majority of the public will agree with one side or the other. If popularity could be used to make a point, debates would be decided before they even started. For example, don't say, "In a national poll, 68% of the public agreed with our perspective" or "The re-election of the present government shows that most people agreed with the war." Such statements do nothing to advance your case.

Using evidence as an argument. While evidence should be used to *support* arguments, it shouldn't be used to *form* arguments. Examples and statistics provide backup for key points, but they aren't contentious points themselves. If what you're saying is a fact, then it isn't debatable. And if it isn't debatable, then it isn't an argument. Stating, "The Affirmative's first argument is that there were 1,250 murders in the city last year, which is up 11% from the year before" is a piece of evidence, not an argument.

Evoking a famous person's views. Certainly, the views of a statesman or a celebrity may be acceptable if they add reasoned, substantive support to an argument. Unfortunately, this technique is often misused. For example, some debaters will make a statement like, "The Negative's case is correct because in 2004, our perspective was endorsed by ..." So what? For the same reason that public opinion shouldn't be employed, endorsements don't have a place either. Remember, a debate is about how *you* argue for or against the resolution, not what someone else happens to think about the issue.

Basing a point on legality. Some debaters will use laws, particularly constitutions, to argue the validity of the *principle* behind an argument. However, rules and regulations aren't substitutes for reasoned arguments. Except if clearly stated in the resolution, a debate isn't about the legality of a particular practice. Even if a practice is illegal, the debate could focus on whether it *should* be illegal. It's possible to make principled arguments for both sides of a law. For example, you shouldn't say, "The Negative's second argument is that Section 9.3a of the national constitution implies that media censorship is wrong."

Supporting a practice because it's a choice. Just because a practice is an option, it doesn't make it more right or more wrong. Say you're debating that governments should allow public-private partnerships for national parks management. It would be poor form to argue, "The government gets to choose on a case by case basis whether a partnership is a good idea. If it's good, there will be a partnership. If it isn't, there won't be a partnership. Since it's a choice, our opponent's harms can't possibly exist." You should have argued that, on balance, these partnerships *are* a good idea, not that they *may* be a good idea.

Building a chain of arguments. Developing points as a series of progressive reasons, each argument building on the previous argument, is a tempting tactic. It allows you to show the logical development of your perspective. Unfortunately, it's often very risky. If you construct a chain of arguments and your opponent is able to break a single link in the chain, your entire case may fall apart. Don't feel that you shouldn't ever use dependent arguments, but think carefully about this risk before you do so.

POINTS ARE BRANDS, AND BRANDS HAVE LABELS

How does a company take a product with many features and benefits and present it in a way that's easy to for consumers to grasp? It creates a brand, and then it labels the product so that it instantly catches your eye. Debating points should be treated in a similar way. You may have spent several minutes talking about the reasons, support, and implications concerning a point. How is a judge to recall exactly what argument it was or what it meant? Simple: label it.

> **Success Tip!**
>
> When you 'brand' your points, make the labels easy to remember.

Suppose that your second constructive point explains how creating a new education agency would lead to major staffing problems, wasted resources, and countless delays. This is your "messy bureaucracy" point. Or, say your argument is that television shows and magazines have created unhealthy and socially harmful views of how a young girl should look, leading many teenagers to have poor eating habits and low self-esteem. This is your "image stereotype" point. Not only does this strategy make it easier for others to digest and remember what you've said, it also makes it easier for you to refer back to your points later on in the debate.

THE POLICY PROCESS

If you're the Affirmative team in a policy debate, you have to establish *why* there needs to be change and *what* you plan to do about it. If you're the Negative team, your case will usually include arguments in favor of the current system.

In practice, a plan is a thorough set of procedures and rationales that takes many hours or hundreds of pages to explain. Unfortunately, you're considerably limited in a debate. Your challenge is to present a plan concisely, while communicating the key aspects effectively. Here are some strategies for building strong plans:

Stick to a few steps. Just as it's tough for judges to digest more than a few arguments, it's equally difficult to comprehend a plan with too many steps. Usually, having three parts in your plan is a good rule of thumb, perhaps one more or one less if the situation warrants. If your plan has five or six points, you're likely to confuse the judges. Stating only one step makes your plan seem incomplete.

Strike a good balance between general and specific. Granted, this is tricky. You don't want to speak in such generalities that nobody knows what exactly you want to do. At the same time, it's not necessary to get into small details. Say you're calling for graduated, multi-stage driver licensing. Here's a comparison to illustrate the concept of balance:

• *Too general*: "We would have tests for each stage of licensing."

• *Too specific*: "At Stage 1, we would implement a 25 question multiple choice knowledge test and a 30 minute road test focusing on five key areas of driving proficiency. In addition, the following six conditions would be placed on Stage 1 drivers under the age of 18 ..."

• *Good balance*: "At Stage 1, there would be a written knowledge test and a practical road test. At Stage 2, there would only be a road test, but it would be more challenging and more comprehensive than the previous road test."

Fit the plan with the needs for change. Your plan should be an extension of your needs for change, solving directly and effectively the problems that you brought up. Many debaters present plans that are very solid in their own right, but with advantages and rationales that are significantly different than the needs for change discussed previously. When you state your plan, it's helpful to explain exactly how your proposal solves the problems in the present system.

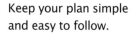

Success Tip!

Keep your plan simple and easy to follow.

Use language that's easy to comprehend. Presenting a plan shouldn't be akin to playing the role of a lawyer. You should avoid using complex, legalistic language that sounds like formal legislation. Make sure that your judges will be able to understand your plan easily and quickly.

Don't spend too much time on it. Although a plan is an important part of policy debate, it should rarely become the central focus. Overly technical debates centering on implementation issues get very dry. The primary focus should be on why the system needs to change, and the plan should largely clarify how, in a broad sense, you would go about carrying out the changes in an effective and efficient way.

CRITERIA TO LAY DOWN THE YARDSTICKS

In most instances, the definition does a reasonably good job of clearing up what the debate is about. By defining the terms how it chooses, the Affirmative team is explaining what it has to prove and telling the Negative team that it has to show the opposite.

However, a team can setup criteria to examine more specifically what each side needs to prove in order to win. There are two main goals that a team may want to achieve by using criteria:

Goal #1: To provide a 'litmus test' for the judges. In many values debates, two teams may argue very persuasively why a resolution is true or false, but both have entirely different interpretations of what needs to be proven. One or both teams may find it helpful to lay out the criteria by which the judges should decide who won.

Suppose that the debate is on the resolution, "Resolved: the United Nations is a failure." The Affirmative defines the topic as "the Security Council failing to deliver international peace and security." How do we know what's considered a "failure." What do we mean by "peace and security?" The Affirmative could set two criteria: *solving* crises it could have solved, and *discouraging* wars and civil conflicts.

Goal #2: As a high-risk strategy to stake out the core issues. Ideally, the debate will center around your preferred issues. Most teams will say from the outset what they think the debate is about, and they'll plead their case again in the rebuttal speech. Laying out criteria is the most explicit way to mark your territory. However, it also paints a big target on your back. If the other team can show the judges that you haven't met all of the criteria that you created, it's far less likely that you'll win the debate.

Say you're the Affirmative team for the resolution, "Be it resolved that the law society should select federal judges." You could claim that there are two criteria for deciding the issue: the process must be *objective*, and the selection must be based solely on legal *merit*. Clearly, you feel that your team has the upper hand on both accounts. However, if the Negative team can raise enough doubt about the law society's objectivity, the judges may decide that you lost the debate even if your overall case was strong.

Your decision on whether to use criteria should be based on how confident you are that you can meet them. There's nothing worse than proposing a set of criteria, only to see your opponent use your own words against you. Here are some strategies to follow if you decide to go with this case strategy:

Present them at the beginning of your first speech. It's only fair that your opponent knows your version of the criteria at the outset. This allows its speakers to clash with your case accordingly or to argue for a different set of criteria.

Don't confuse criteria with arguments. A set of criteria is a tool with which to *evaluate* your arguments, but they aren't actually arguments themselves. Using the judge selection example discussed previously, it would be weak to say, "Our first point is that the law society is more objective, which addresses our first criterion." There's no distinction here between the criterion and the argument. On the other hand, you could say, "The Affirmative's first argument is that the law society would not receive any direct benefit as a result of its choices, which meets our criteria of *objectivity* and *merit*."

Use only a few criteria. Stating two criteria is typical, and three criteria should be the maximum. The more criteria you use, the more angles of attack you give to your opponents and the more you have to prove. If you use greater than three, you'll be complicating the debate and making it difficult for you to show how your points collectively meet all of the criteria. Imagine asking your judges to understand how five constructive points each meet four criteria! You would confuse even the most experienced judge.

Link your arguments back to the criteria. Many teams will boldly state a set of criteria, and then will never refer back to them during the remainder of the debate. The criteria will become less and less relevant as the debate continues. Worse yet, the judges could remember the criteria (they probably wrote them down), but be left wondering if you actually met them. As you deliver arguments and present your rebuttal, it's important you show that what you're saying is directly meeting the criteria you put forth initially.

Prove each condition in each speech. It's usually not a good idea to divide your case based on criteria. For instance, you shouldn't have the first speaker address the first measure and the second speaker prove the second one. The criteria are markers by which your *entire* case will be judged. Therefore, both speakers should refer to the full set of criteria in their respective speeches.

COUNTERING WITH A COUNTER PLAN

In a policy debate, it seems common sense that the Negative should refute every point brought forth by the Affirmative. Namely, it should clash with the professed needs for changing the system and the Affirmative's plan for carrying out the changes. Some teams, though, prefer to use one of the most risky tactics available: the counter plan.

What exactly is a counter plan? It's case strategy in which the Negative team agrees with the Affirmative's needs for change, but argues for a different plan to act on the deficiencies in the present system. The debate focuses not on the principled arguments for or against change. It focuses instead on which team has a more effective plan to deal with the situation.

Not all judges like counter plans. Rather than creating debates on competing principles, counter plan cases often become technical, speculative cases on which proposal would be more suitable. For this reason, counter plans are the most misused type of Negative case strategy. If you're thinking of using a counter plan, there are two requirements that it must meet:

Requirement #1: The counter plan must be significantly different from the Affirmative's plan. A debate is supposed to be between two opposites. If you've already conceded that the Affirmative's needs for change are correct, the gap between the two teams has been narrowed considerably. A counter plan that merely enhances or presents minor differences to the Affirmative's proposal is inappropriate. It must be fundamentally distinct from the Affirmative's plan so that there's a clear gulf between the two sides.

For example, let's take a case on whether the United Nations should impose sanctions on a country that's abusing human rights. The Affirmative team discusses the severity of the crimes committed and recommends a series of economic sanctions. Here's a poor counter plan strategy: "We agree that the United Nations must deal with these human rights abuses, but we believe that political sanctions in addition to economic sanctions would be a more effective plan." This counter plan isn't all that distinct from the Affirmative's case.

A more effective Negative strategy could be the following: "We will show you why economic sanctions are insufficient. We will instead propose the threat of military force if the abuses are not stopped immediately." Is this risky? Certainly. But it would be valid counter plan because you now have a contentious debate between economic and military solutions.

Requirement #2: It must be significantly more practical or effective. Sounds obvious, right? Unfortunately, many Negative teams present a counter plan that may be very different from the Affirmative's plan, but that reaches a relatively similar outcome. It's not enough to say that your plan "will get us slightly closer to the desired results" or "is less risky and less prone to abuses than the Affirmative's plan." You must be able to prove that your plan is the *only* one that will work effectively and that the Affirmative's plan will fail outright.

A counter plan has major implications for the Negative's responsibility in the debate. In a typical debate, the burden of proof lies largely with the Affirmative. The Affirmative must prove that its needs for change are valid and that its plan is effective, whereas the Negative can technically win if it raises sufficient doubts concerning the Affirmative's case. If a counter plan is employed, both teams are on an even footing when it comes to burden. The Negative is now required to prove the effectiveness of its proposals. In fact, even though both teams carry this burden, most judges will expect more from the Negative, because it chose to take the unorthodox strategy of presenting a counter plan.

The decision to use a counter plan should be considered very carefully. It's highly recommended that only experienced debaters try this approach. There are simply too many pitfalls for a beginner to venture into this uncharted territory.

If you feel that you're ready to take up the counter plan, make sure that the situation is ripe for this risky strategy. The best instance to use a counter plan is when the Affirmative's needs for change are so strong that you would be at a disadvantage trying to debate them. By conceding that the stated needs are common sense, you're essentially telling your judges that the Affirmative hasn't presented anything bold or insightful in its first speech.

A counter plan can be effective at throwing off your opponent. The second Affirmative speaker usually has to discard most of his or her speech and come up with a new one on the fly. Used effectively, a counter plan can add a dimension of surprise and sophistication to the debate. Used poorly, it can leave the judges shaking their heads at your failure to hit the core issues of the round.

HAVING A GOOD (CASE) BREAKUP

You've developed four to six powerful, well-developed arguments. Now the challenge is to divide the points between the two constructive speeches. The way that you 'split' your arguments is an important decision from an organizational and a strategic perspective. A sound division enhances the structure and coherency of your case. It also has implications for how the debate unfolds.

Hasty and Hazardous Splits

Let's start with what *not* to do when dividing your points between speeches (they've been done far too often to ignore):

First speaker outlines, second speaker expands. Wouldn't it be easier simply to let the first debater present the entire case, so that the judges have a clear picture right from the beginning? Sure, if you want to let the other team stab away at poorly supported arguments. While it's a good idea for the second speaker to defend against refutation of your team's fully developed points, it's a tall order to depend on your partner to defend or expand on an poorly supported point that's already been torn apart.

Arguments are divided randomly. Your strategy should be deliberate and thoughtful. A random split between partners leaves your case looking scattered. It makes as much sense as a sports team randomly deciding who should play each position.

Each person delivers his or her favorite points. It's certainly tempting to let each team member deliver the points that he or she likes the most. Logically, you may be more effective if you're passionate about the points. While it may help you make excellent *arguments*, it will probably also lead to a poor *case*. Like a random split, if there's no logical basis for the type of division selected, the risk is that your case will appear disorganized.

The 'meat' is left to the second speaker. Even though both team members should work together to build a case, each speech should *independently* support your side of the resolution. Say you're arguing that the Olympics are too commercialized. The first speaker talks about the extent to which they are commercialized, and the second speaker says why this level of commercialization is bad—the heart of the case. This is called a 'hung case' because the first speaker has not said anything explaining why the Olympics are "*too* commercialized."

The Best Breakups

Now that you know how not to split your case, what is the best split strategy? Usually, it involves dividing your case into themes or categories of your central theme. Since every case is different, each one requires a unique, tailored approach. Here are a few good options:

National and international. Many cases have implications both at home and abroad, such as international economic, military, and legal issues. Say you're debating whether your country should sign a particular environmental treaty. One speaker could focus on the impact within your nation's borders, and the other speaker could emphasize the international benefits or why signing the agreement fits with your nation's place in the world.

Short-term and long-term. If the debate is on a values topic, you could split your points between the immediate and future harms of the circumstance. For example, the first speaker could discuss how spanking a child causes short-term harm, and the second speaker could describe the long-term impact on a child's development.

If the debate is on a policy topic, it may make sense to split the arguments based on short-term and long-term outcomes. If you're debating whether a particular country should be attacked, the short-term theme could be the 'peace and security' impact, and the long-term theme could be the 'democracy and human rights' impact.

Society and individual. This type of split is particularly useful when a situation or policy impacts both an individual's life and the way society operates. If the debate is about banning the use of cell phones while driving, one speaker could discuss the positive impact on an individual's ability to drive carefully, and the other speaker could focus on how everyone would be safer as a result.

Economic and social. While the 'society and individual' split is based on *who* is affected, this split technique focuses largely on what aspect of society is impacted. This same concept works for military and political, cultural and economic, and a variety of such combinations. Let's take a case in favor of government subsidies for the arts. The first speaker could focus on social benefits, such as increasing community enjoyment of museums and theatres. The second speaker could focus on economic benefits, such as keeping struggling industries alive and saving thousands of vital jobs.

As mentioned previously, don't rely solely on these common splits. They're noted primarily to spark some ideas. The best splits are case-specific. These are a few examples of more narrow splits that apply to particular debate cases:

- **Violence on television**: young children and school environment
- **Mandatory minimum sentences**: criminals and victims
- **Media concentration**: editorial slant and information diversity
- **Televised trials**: right to know and ability to scrutinize
- **Required vaccinations**: public health and personal health

Once you've decided on the split, which one comes first? While there's no definitive rule, think about which theme forms the foundation of your case. If the main thrust of your case is the impact on individuals, and the impact on society is an *extension* of the influence on people, you should probably put the 'individual' theme first. It's tempting to leave your key points to the end, allowing less time for your opponent to refute them. However, there are three reasons why presenting them earlier is usually the best option:

Set the tone for the debate. By presenting your most important arguments first, you're signaling to the judges that they are the core, deciding issues of the debate.

Maintain attention throughout. When you present an argument early, it's more likely to be refuted and defended several times. This creates a logical extension into the rebuttal, when you can show how your core arguments have won the round.

Be seen as hitting the key issues. On any topic, most judges will have at least some expectation of what the most important issues are. You don't want it to seem that you've missed the crux of the debate.

ORDERLY ORGANIZATION

Thoughtful organization is essential to the success of your case. Without a strong structure, your case is simply an assortment of points that lacks a clear sense of direction. You'll be more effective if you present the points with a carefully designed arrangement.

Within each point, the "Claim, Comment, Cite, Conclude" rule discussed in Chapter 4 is a good rule of thumb to follow. It allows you to address, in order, the four elements that a judge wants to hear: a brief *statement* of what the argument is, an *explanation* of why it's correct, some *evidence* to backup the explanation, and a *closing* that reinforces the impact of the argument.

As for the overall speech, it's helpful to follow the rule also explained in Chapter 4: "Tell them what you're going to tell them, then tell them, then tell them what you told them." The "tell them" part is simply your arguments, and the "tell them what you told them" part is a brief wrap up of your arguments and a tie back to your theme at the end of your speech. When you "tell them what you're going to tell them," make sure that you're not too general. The more clearly you state where you plan to go with your speech, the more your judges will understand and look forward to what you have to say. Then again, you don't want to give away your entire case before you've delved fully into the arguments. Here's a comparison:

• *Too general*: "First, I'm going to refute what the first Affirmative speaker said. Second, I'm going to present the Negative's case." You haven't told the judges anything tangible. Rather, you've told them in the most general sense how you'll be organizing your speech.

• *Too specific*: "First, I'm going to refute the Affirmative's case by citing a 2003 report which invalidates its first point, then I'm going to explain the faulty cause and effect relationship in the example used to support its second point ..." You'll get to all of these details when you actually refute the points. This is far too specific for the judges to digest at the opening of your speech. Your goal should be to provide an *overview* of what you're going to say.

• *Good balance*: "First, I'm going to refute the Affirmative's case by explaining how its proposal to elect judges would weaken the impartiality of the legal system. Second, I'm going to introduce the Negative's case by telling you why appointed judges are less beholden to any political or interest group." This level of detail paints a clear picture of where you're going, without completely revealing the specifics.

CHANGING ON THE FLY

It's every debater's worst nightmare. The topic has been announced months before the tournament. You've prepared extensively for both sides of the debate. Then unexpectedly, as the debate begins, the first Affirmative speaker presents a perfectly reasonable definition that makes your case irrelevant.

What should you do? Many debaters will decide to argue against the definition. They do so not because it's unfair, but so that they can fit their long-prepared case into the round. There's a sense—a false sense—that as long as they present exceptional arguments, they can get away with their own definition of the resolution. As discussed in Chapter 6, this tactic should be avoided at all costs. If the Affirmative's definition is reasonable, you have to follow it.

Other debaters will just ignore the definition altogether and continue with their case anyways. This only marginalizes the Negative team, as the judges will be perplexed that it's debating a significantly different issue. There will essentially be two separate debates going on, and an astute judge will assign blame to the Negative team for trying to bypass the definition.

The best teams will swallow their pride and forget their long nights of preparation. They'll take comfort in realizing that their preparation was a great learning experience, and that it made them familiar with the issue. And then they'll abandon much or all of their case. Yes, the most effective teams will *abandon* their case only minutes

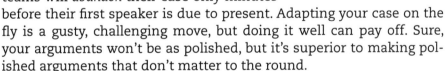

Success Tip!

If your case doesn't fit, fix it or nix it.

before their first speaker is due to present. Adapting your case on the fly is a gusty, challenging move, but doing it well can pay off. Sure, your arguments won't be as polished, but it's superior to making polished arguments that don't matter to the round.

If you've made the decision to change your case on the fly, you have to act quickly and decisively. Within the span of a few minutes, you need not only to listen carefully to your opponent's speech, but also to come up with new constructive arguments. How can you adapt confidently and effectively?

Don't panic. Many debaters spend valuable time fretting about the seemingly daunting task that lies ahead. They say to their partner,

"Oh my, what on earth are we going to do about this?" You should be thinking, "We *can* do this, now let's figure out *how*."

Start with refutation. Don't stop listening to what's being said. Keep on using your flow sheet and thinking about how you'll refute the Affirmative's points. If you blank out completely and can't think of constructive points, at least you can clash with your opponent's points for the majority or all of your speaking time.

Turn refutation into construction. If you can't think of original arguments, try basing them on your refutation. When you're clashing with a point, you're taking a stand saying that a principle is *wrong*. Logically, then, you believe that something else—likely the opposite perspective—is *right*. And arguing for what you think is right is the starting point for constructive matter. Use this thought process if you find yourself stuck at the last minute.

Divide responsibilities. The second Negative speaker doesn't have to worry about clash right away, so he or she can focus on coming up with constructive arguments. This allows the first Negative speaker to listen carefully to the first Affirmative speaker and to plan effective refutation. Late in the first Affirmative speech, the second Negative speaker can 'pass on' the proposed arguments to his or her partner.

"SWOT" YOUR CASE

Once you've developed a case, it's a good idea to take a step back and think about how you can improve it. When you were building the case, your perspective was that of a *constructor*. After you've done so, analyze your case with an eye of a *renovator*. Your task is to take what's already prepared and to enhance it. The most effective way to strengthen your case and to plug any gaping holes is to do a "SWOT" analysis: *Strengths, Weaknesses, Opportunities,* and *Threats*.

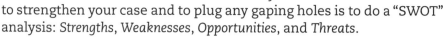

> **Success Tip!**
>
> Strengthen your case by asking a friend to criticize it.

• **Strengths**. What arguments have you developed well? Evaluate your points and think about which ones are the most convincing, effectively explained, and appropriately supported. These are your strengths—

the pillars of your case. You should emphasize them in your speeches and ensure that they become the deciding issues of the round.

• **Weaknesses**. Do you have any arguments that aren't particularly convincing or that have insufficient explanation and support? If so, one possible response is to get rid of the points entirely, especially if the argument itself is weak. If the argument happens to be strong but the detail surrounding it is weak, spend some time expanding on the point and clarifying its rationales.

• **Opportunities**. What haven't you said that could be effective? Think about the case from different angles. Brainstorm more ideas. If you've missed an opportunity that would boost your case, make the necessary additions or modifications.

• **Threats**. Are there arguments that have obvious and potentially damaging counter-arguments? Of course, no constructive point is beyond criticism. But if in the process of critiquing your points, you find yourself struggling to defend them against possible counter-arguments, you need to take action. Think about what you would say in response to refutation, and don't hesitate to discard an argument completely if you can't find a solid defense.

'CASE' STUDY: WAR CRIMES TRIBUNALS VS. TRUTH AND RECONCILIATION COMMISSIONS

In this section, we're going to take a look at both an Affirmative case and a Negative case on the resolution, "Be it resolved that Truth and Reconciliation Commissions should be favored over War Crimes Tribunals." A War Crimes Tribunal aims to bring the perpetrators of war crimes to justice following a civil or international conflict. Examples include the International Criminal Court (ICC) and the International Criminal Tribunal for Rwanda (ICTR). A Truth and Reconciliation Commission strives to help society heal, without exacting punishment on the offenders. Examples include the 1995 South Africa commission and the 2002 East Timor commission.

Let's start by taking a look at how the Affirmative could build a case. To start the case development process, it's a good idea to identify the core themes. The first theme could be the *practical effectiveness of* a Truth and Reconciliation Commission in uncovering the truth. The second theme could be the positive *impact on people*, including individuals and families affected directly by the conflict and society as a whole. These pillars also serve as an appropriate way to split arguments between the two speakers. Here's a possible structure and series of arguments, including labels, for the Affirmative's case:

Affirmative Speaker #1
Theme: "Practical Effectiveness"

1. *Uncovering facts.* Truth and Reconciliation Commissions are more effective at developing a factual account of the truth, because victims and perpetrators alike have incentives and opportunities to tell their stories. In War Crimes Tribunals, defendants often seek to hide information and to distort the truth.

2. *Greater feasibility.* Truth and Reconciliation Commissions are more feasible to implement than War Crimes Tribunals. Nations ravished by war usually don't have a strong, independent judiciary and legal system for the purpose of prosecuting wartime offenders.

3. *Useful recommendations.* The commissions are effective at producing useful recommendations to ensure that such situations don't occur in the future. War Crimes Tribunals are concerned primarily with punishment, not with education and improvement.

Affirmative Speaker #2
Theme: "Impact on People"

1. *Emotional healing.* Revealing the truth is essential to the psychological healing process. People need to know what happened and who was responsible, so that they can reach a feeling of closure. War Crimes Tribunals can be adversarial to the point of sparking anger.

2. *Social unity.* Truth and Reconciliation Commissions aim to unify society, whereas War Crimes Tribunals may be seen as instruments of revenge. This unity also aids in the establishment of a new, democratic government with the legitimacy and credibility necessary to represent everyone in society.

Now that we've mapped out a possible Affirmative case, let's turn our attention to the Negative side. Like the Affirmative, it's best to start with the core themes of the case. The first theme could focus on the *immediate* benefits of a War Crimes Tribunal. The second theme could emphasize the *overall* impact. Below are some of the arguments that could be brought forth as part of the Negative's case:

Negative Speaker #1
Theme: "Immediate Impact"

1. *Disband aggressors.* War Crimes Tribunals serve to disband and diminish the power of the militant groups that committed the violent acts. This makes it far more difficult for them to resume or continue their wartime atrocities.

2. *Sense of resolution.* Victims of wartime atrocities will only feel a sense of resolution when those responsible for the war crimes are found guilty and punished. It's important for victims to know that blame has been assigned to specific individuals.

Negative Speaker #2
Theme: "Overall Message"

1. *Deters future abuses.* War Crimes Tribunals send an overall message to potential future offenders that such acts will not be tolerated. Without such tribunals, there won't be sufficient disincentive against these types of criminal actions.

2. *International standards.* War Crimes Tribunals are a move toward internationally recognized standards of human rights, such as the International Criminal Court. Therefore, they send an overall signal that those who commit wartime atrocities will be punished irrespective of national boundaries or differing legal standards.

3. *Moral obligation.* In general, there is a moral obligation to punish war criminals, in accordance with basic principles of humanity. Allowing amnesty violates fundamental human values, essentially condoning or ignoring such crimes.

You probably noticed that there's a partial match between the themes of each team's first speaker. They focused largely on the practical impact and effectiveness of the respective systems. However, the second speakers had fairly different themes, which is quite normal. Each team is trying to focus its arguments and the split of these points between partners in a way that it feels serves its interests.

This chapter discussed how to develop strong, convincing arguments around clear and logical themes, regardless of the type of resolution you're debating. It also mentioned important tips to remember when you're dividing points between partners. If you follow these guidelines, your debate cases will be significantly stronger.

CHAPTER 8
Clash with Impact:
Mastering the Art of the Attack

Coming Up!

Once you've built a solid case, the next step is figuring out how to challenge your opponent's case. In this chapter, you'll learn about the multiple ways to clash with the other team's points during constructive speeches, and how to complete an overall attack in the rebuttal.

TAKING THE LEAP: THE CHALLENGE OF REFUTATION

Without clash between the two teams, a debate would simply be a collection of speeches. Competitors would be able to plan and practice the entire debate beforehand, and there wouldn't be any back and forth flow of arguments. The focus would be on making a great *speech*, rather than contributing to a great *debate*. Remember, though, that debate isn't only about proving that you're right. It's also about proving that the other team is wrong.

Clash, or refutation, is the process of countering point by point the arguments brought forth by the other team. Your purpose is to be critical and to raise doubts in the minds of the judges. Effective clash will force your opponent to go on the defensive and to rebuild its case.

Many debaters, especially beginners, find refutation particularly difficult. Why? Quite simply, it's the part of a debate that you can't plan in advance. But what if you make mistakes? Isn't it more effective to use prepared, practiced text and to deliver it flawlessly? The reality is actually the opposite. You'll be in a superior position if you devote significant effort to clash, even if your clash has mistakes and weaknesses. Since you're unable to plan your refutation, you're not expected to be as fluent as when you present your own team's case.

Even though you can't plan your clash precisely, you can make yourself familiar with the general tools of refutation. That is, you can learn about the variety of angles from which to clash with an opponent's case. This will prepare you to spot such opportunities quickly when they come up in a round. You can also anticipate some of the ideas that the other team may bring up and consider how you would go about challenging them.

TO REFUTE OR NOT TO REFUTE?

Before diving into *how* to refute, it's important to know *what* to refute. The short explanation is that you should refute any part of your opponent's case that's important in proving its side of the resolution. While this advice may seem self-evident, much of any team's case is extra information that 'pads' the most important elements. You won't be

Success Tip!

Clash with every relevant point made by your opponent.

able to refute everything, so knowing what's essential and what isn't can make your clash significantly stronger.

Usually, you should stick to the core of each of your opponent's points—the single sentence that outlines the argument—and the logical analysis and explanation that follows. It's important to do this for every argument, as you don't want to leave any important points untouched. However, there are some areas that you should generally aim to avoid in your clash:

Process and technique. Refutation should focus exclusively on substantive matter. For instance, if a speaker goes over time, don't take up any of your time telling the judges about it. You may also come across debaters who present poorly structured speeches, but you shouldn't try to convince the judges of this weakness. Finally, you should avoid comments on how effectively the other team debated, such as saying, "The first Negative speaker showed poor skill in explaining her second point." It's up to the judges to decide how well each person debated.

Case theme. Surely, the purpose of your speech is to show why your opponent's theme is incorrect. But you shouldn't try to do so by debating that the theme itself is wrong, as it's too broad to be refuted directly. A theme is a grouping and summary of a series of arguments, each of which addresses a specific issue. Your goal in refutation is to weaken the theme by targeting the individual arguments. It may also be useful to explain how your critique of a particular point has damaged your opponent's case theme.

Sources and statistics. Addressing the usefulness of your opponent's evidence or pointing out a factual inaccuracy can add some value to your clash. That being said, a common mistake is trying to argue against sources and statistics directly, rather than the points themselves. "Our source is better than your source" or "We have better statistics" types of counter-arguments do little to refute the arguments that form the basis of the other team's case. Evidence *illustrates* an argument but doesn't make or break an argument.

THE TOOLS OF TERRIFIC CLASH

There are countless angles from which to clash with your opponent's case. This section presents a few of the more common ones, which will give you a general idea of how to approach the attack. You can certainly delve into the many books and articles devoted to more technical refutation concepts. Such concepts go by names like "post hoc fallacy" and "non sequitur." If you don't have any clue what these phrases mean, don't worry. Most debaters don't. While it may be useful to know about them as you become an advanced debater, you can get quite far by understanding the tools discussed in this section.

Issue Challenges

Said correctly, a challenge will double as clash by implying what's wrong with the argument. It takes less time to issue a challenge that to counter a point directly. By spending a few seconds telling the other team what specifically it has to prove, you're forcing it to spend valuable time responding to the challenge. It's efficient for you and inefficient for your opponent.

Success Tip!

When issuing a challenge, explain why it's important.

When making a challenge, be confident and decisive in how you present it. For example, start with, "The Affirmative must prove ..." or "A fundamental assumption that the Opposition has to explain is ..." In doing so, you'll simultaneously signal to your judges that a particular issue must be addressed and to your opponents that they have to deal with it. These are some examples of how to issue a challenge:

• **Media influence**: "There's a fundamental question that the Affirmative must answer in order to justify its case that the news media has a negative influence on society. How else would we receive vital information about emergencies, such as hurricanes and earthquakes?"

• **Environmental standards**: "The 'black hole' in the Affirmative's plan must be addressed in the second speaker's speech. How will the government convince people to practice the proposed environmental standards, if there's no reasonable way to monitor violations?"

Attack Assumptions

Most arguments rest on one or more assumptions. Often, these assumptions appear normal, so it's unlikely a team will spend significant time justifying them. One way of clashing is to attack these assumptions, weakening the foundation for the point. It's also important that you explain why the assumption in question is central to the rest of the team's case. Here are two examples of targeting a team's assumptions:

Success Tip!

Explain how a false assumption damages the entire case.

• **ID cards**: "The Affirmative's suggestion that we should ask everyone for ID to prove they're over age 18 assumes that the ID presented is genuine. It's easy for young people to get a fake ID, which damages the viability of its plan."

• **Post-secondary funding**: "The Negative's argument that we need to pay for more of students' post-secondary education assumes that some student debt is necessarily a bad thing. It actually forces students to budget and spend carefully, and it makes them work hard after graduation to establish a solid financial base."

Break Links

Imagine a friend said to you, "Inexpensive air travel means more time spent outside cities, which means less smog affecting cities, which means lower health care costs, which means lower taxes, which means a stronger economy, which means less property crime. So, if the government was serious about making us feel safer, it would subsidize airline tickets." You can probably think of a handful of places where your friend made weak links to arrive at this ridiculous conclusion.

Granted, you probably won't see a chain this fragile in a debate. But you may see a team present a series of two or three arguments that are closely related or that depend on each other. Sometimes this strategy creates a cause and effect link. One point is the reason, and another point is the implication. You can clash with linked arguments together by attacking the stated or implied connection between points, claiming that it's weak or that it doesn't exist. Here are two examples of clashing with arguments by breaking links:

• **Student performance**: "Our opponent's second point claimed that lower performance in our district's schools is a result of the first point, namely students spending too much time on video games and Internet chat. In reality, a variety of factors impact student performance, such as economic trends, political decisions, and school management. More time spent on these non-academic distractions may actually be a symptom of these other influences."

• **Income taxes**: "The Affirmative started by arguing that eliminating patents for medicines would allow more firms to manufacture drugs. In its second point, it falsely implied that this would increase drug discovery. If we reduce the profit motive by disallowing patents, then in fact fewer firms would take part in drug discovery."

Indicate Irrelevance

It may not be necessary to spend significant time saying why a point is wrong if you can show why it doesn't matter even if it's right. In some cases, an argument may hit at an issue that's well outside the scope of the definition, and at other times, it may be insignificant to your opponent's case theme. Your goal is to 'take the point out of the round' by making it seem like your opponent was wasting its time by even bringing up the argument. Here are some examples:

• **Standardized tests**: "The Negative's third constructive point argued that too much testing *in general* adversely impacts young students. The point is irrelevant, as the issue here is whether the *standardization* of the tests across schools is harmful. For most students, the absence of a standardized test would simply mean having to write a school-developed exam in its place."

• **Media funding**: "In making its case that our publicly-funded broadcaster should be privatized, the Affirmative's second argument was that maximum choice is in the public interest. This is an irrelevant point, because privatization would only change the structure and nature of this one organization, not the *number* of broadcasters."

Unfortunately, many debaters misuse this tool of refutation. In each of the cases below, the guise of claiming irrelevance is being used in order to avoid hitting the issue directly:

"It's simply unrelated." Supporting an argument with information from another time period or another place is a common and potentially useful tactic. Of course, it may very well be the case that the analogy is a poor one. Unfortunately, rather than claiming irrelevance only for weak comparisons, some debaters will try to exclude a point simply because it's from a situation outside the core debate. Suppose the Affirmative says, "The success of the Swedish model of public health care shows why we should adopt it in this country." One could think of many reasons why this analogy doesn't really prove the point of the debate. A weak response, though, would be to say, "Well, that's just Sweden, and we're not talking about Sweden."

"It's just an exception." Simply saying that an argument or example is "an exception to the usual circumstance" or that "it's really just an isolated point" doesn't get to the heart of *why* it isn't relevant to the round. Say that on a debate about the entertainment media's influence, the Affirmative argues that "foul language on many television shows leads to more swearing at school." The Negative can't just say that "the Affirmative's point is an exception, because not all children's shows are like that." The Affirmative isn't trying to prove that all entertainment media has a negative influence, but only that *on balance* a negative influence *exists*.

Catch Contradictions

Since a sound case is consistent, demonstrating inconsistencies either within a speech or between partners can do serious damage to your opponent's arguments. You'll usually notice a contradiction fairly quickly, and the inconsistency will be apparent to everyone concerned. So while it's a good idea to point it out, don't take up too much time dwelling on it. You can actually force the other team to take up some of its time in the next speech by asking that it explain what its 'real' position is. Below are two examples of catching contradictions:

• **School locker searches**: "The Affirmative's first speaker said that searches by school officials or police officers are justified because school lockers are school property, but the second speaker said that searches are a reasonable intrusion into an area that she clearly stated was a student's private property. Which one is it, public or private?"

• **Health care privatization**: "My opponent's first point was that a publicly-funded system allows equal, timely access to every member of society. Then, in her second point, she argued that only in a system that's publicly-funded could patients receive quicker treatment or be asked to wait on medical grounds alone. If this is the case, then it's clearly not 'equal' and 'timely' for everyone, but just for those people the authorities decide should go first."

Counter Correlations

The fact that two circumstances happened together or in sequence doesn't necessarily mean that one *caused* the other. Debaters sometimes use correlation claims to suggest incorrectly the impact of a particular action or circumstance. If clashing on the grounds that one item didn't create the result mentioned, it may be helpful to state what other factors may have caused the outcome. Here are some examples of challenges to correlations:

• **Free trade**: "The first Negative speaker claimed that the slowdown in economic growth is evidence that free trade agreements have been harmful to our country. This statement is clearly unfounded, as we don't know that free trade has caused these tough times. Government policies, oil prices, currency volatility, and a variety of other factors also shape economic performance. In fact, the downturn could have been worse if not for the expansion of trade agreements."

• **School dropout rate**: "We want to challenge the Affirmative's argument that decreased funding for public schools moved lock-step with increased high school dropout rates. The reality is that there are many social and economic factors at play here. The hardship faced by low income families may actually be what's encouraging students to find full-time employment early. It's not necessarily a funding problem."

Make Careful Concessions

Sometimes a point is very clearly true and it makes little sense to refute it. Generally, the fact that it's widely seen as correct makes it a fairly unsophisticated point. Be careful, though, with how you use concessions. Only use them when you're absolutely sure that the point doesn't strengthen your opponent's case. They should never be used because you don't have time to explain your counter-argument more fully or want to focus on other issues. If you concede a point that may not seem vital at the time, your opponent could try to make it more important as the debate goes on. You'll have shut yourself out on any point that you've already conceded. Below is analysis of two instances of making concessions, one effective and one ineffective:

• **School uniforms**: Say a team argues that uniforms "eliminate choice regarding how students express themselves through fashion." Well, of course a *standard* uniform eliminates choice. But is that really the essence of a debate on whether the overall outcome is good or bad? Concede the point and indicate that you want to move on to more important and contentious issues. Don't try to explain the intricacies of how "there are different types of uniforms" or that "the way some-one 'wears' the clothes is itself a form of expression."

• **Political term limits**: Say your opponent contends that term limits would guarantee "more constant change in our political leadership and in our legislative system." You concede, "Of course there would be more change if you impose term limits, so let's move on to the points that are actually in dispute." This may allow your opponent to make a theme of fostering "fresh, innovate policies" a central part of its case. Your team may have been better off arguing why rotating the people in charge doesn't necessarily result in different decisions, or that change isn't always desirable.

Face the Facts

You've read previously that it's normally not effective to clash with the evidence itself. What can be effective is clashing against the *use* of the evidence. A common way to attack evidence is arguing that it doesn't prove the claim. A team may have overstretched an isolated example to represent a wider trend, or cited a statistic with a weak connection to the claim it was meant to support. The following examples illustrate this type of refutation:

• **Arts funding**: "The first Negative speaker cited the bankruptcy and closing of *one* theatre as proof that government subsidies are needed to keep such institutions afloat. This certainly doesn't show a broader problem. It could actually have been either mismanagement or unappealing plays that forced this failure."

• **Private schools**: "Citing their higher placement in school rankings was a weak way for the Affirmative team to show why private schools deserve public funding. The first speaker was trying to make a point relating to worthy *principles* by bringing up a poorly connected example concerning practical *results*."

Attach an (Ugly) Label

Your opponent has obviously tried to make each point seem as brilliant as possible, and your task is to suggest the opposite. If your rival labeled a point in one way to help the judges remember it, why not call it by another name so that they see it how you want them to see it? Labeling a point unfavorably is effective and acceptable, but doing so offensively makes you look unreasonable. For example, you could label part of the other team's case as the "government knows best" point if you're trying to criticize how deeply the bureaucracy would be involved in a family decision. However, calling it the "we think that ordinary people are unintelligent, uninformed, and incapable" point is probably pushing it too far. Here are some complete examples of labeling an opponent's point unfavorably as a useful refutation tool:

> **Success Tip!**
>
> Be concise when labeling an opponent's argument.

• **Genetic engineering**: "After the first Affirmative speaker talked about his rationale for limits on genetically-modified farm seed, she went on to describe an elaborate process of consultation after consultation with stakeholders to decide what the regulations should actually be. This was essentially the 'strike a committee' point. Rather than explaining the Affirmative's plan, she simply said, 'Let's strike a committee and the problem will take care of itself.'"

• **Global poverty**: "The second Affirmative speaker's first point was that we should immediately forgive the debts owed by every poor nation. This point could actually be called the 'write a blank check' point. No conditions to ensure government reform, no guarantee that the money saved will be spent well, and no process to determine how much debt relief is a fair amount in each circumstance."

ORGANIZING EACH POINT OF THE BATTLE

Very often, debaters will be highly organized when making their own points, but quite disorganized when clashing with their opponent's points. It is, after all, more challenging to structure an unprepared refutation of a point than to structure a point you've prepared in advance. While there are a number of ways to organize a counter-argument, here's one common method that has proven particularly effective:

1. **What they argued.** Start by making it clear exactly what point you're refuting. It may seem obvious to you, but it's probably not as obvious to everyone else. This step, while vital, can be completed in a brief sentence. Saying, "The Negative's second point was ..." or "I would now like to clash with the Government's third argument, which was that ..." are examples of how you can begin this part.

2. **Why they're wrong.** This part is the 'meat' of the clash, so it should take up the most time. Your goal is to explain completely and effectively why your opponent's point is incorrect. Some of the ways you can start this element include, "This point is incorrect because ..." or "The problem with this argument lies in its assumption that ..."

> **Watch Out!**
>
> Don't just say it's wrong without explaining why it's wrong.

3. **Why it matters.** Once you've shown why the other team's point is false, you should put your clash into context—the 'so what' of your refutation. A great way to accomplish this objective is to tie the clash back to your opponent's case theme. This way, you're making it clear not only that you've defeated a single point, but that you've weakened a key pillar of your opponent's case. For example, you could say, "The flaws in this argument go to the heart of the Affirmative's theme of diversity, because they reveal that ..."

This type of structure makes it easy for your judges to 'check off' that you've clashed with each of your opponent's points. It also gives you a rough template to follow so that as you listen to your opponent's speech, you can simply 'fill in' the three parts of your clash for each point. Even if you don't get a chance to write down notes for every refutation point, having the words "what they argued, why they're wrong, and why it matters" on your page serves as a valuable reminder of what you need to cover.

ENGINEERING THE OVERALL ATTACK

In addition to having a strong structure for each point of your clash, it's also essential that your overall refutation is organized sensibly. This provides a sense of completeness to the refutation and improves the flow of your speech. There are several key questions that you need to consider when designing your refutation strategy:

Where does the refutation fit into the speech?

Like your constructive points, your clash should stay together as a section of your speech. Some debaters prefer to start with clash, while others prefer to build constructive matter first. Both ways are appropriate, and which one you select comes down to personal preference. Each method has unique benefits:

• *Clashing before constructing.* The key benefit of starting with refutation is that your opponent's points are fresh in your mind and in the minds of your judges. Another advantage is that it leaves your opponent's case significantly weakened before you construct your case. You're essentially telling the judges, "We've already shown you why the other team's case has failed to meet its burden, but here are some constructive arguments to prove definitively why we're correct."

• *Clashing after constructing.* Many debaters are more comfortable starting with what they've already prepared. This method gives you confidence early on in your speech. Once you have momentum, it's easier to transition into your refutation. Also, starting with constructive matter immediately shifts the debate back into your court, seizing the agenda from your opponent right at the outset. In addition, if you're short on time and need to make adjustments, it's easier to be selective in your refutation than in your constructive matter.

In what order should you clash?

The easiest, most common sense way to order your clash is to go in the same order as your opponent presented the arguments. This method is less complicated for you, as you can simply go down your flow sheet and fire back at the arguments in the order that they're listed. This is also easy for your judges to follow, because they'll have remembered or recorded them in the same sequence.

However, there are select circumstances when it might make sense to take a different route. Firstly, if a particular point is critical to your opponent's case and damaging it would significantly undermine its core theme, you could consider starting with that argument. Saying, for example, "I want to begin with my opponent's second constructive point. It's the foundation of the Affirmative's case because ..." makes it clear why you're taking this route. (Notice the word "because." You should always say why the point is vital to the debate.) Secondly, if you're concerned that you may run out time, it's preferable to have covered at least the key points.

How do you allocate time to each point?

While it's important to clash with every point, it's not necessary to spend an equal amount of time on each one. If there's a simple, easy to state reason why you feel that a point is wrong, get it across in a few sentences and move on. Leave a greater amount of time for arguments that are more critical or that require more detailed refutation.

If you've already presented additional constructive points, you could decide to shorten a refutation point by stating how you've already covered the crux of your opponent's argument through your own point. For example, if one of your new points is that "forgiving the debts owed by poor countries will speed up government reform," you could refer back to this point when refuting your opponent's argument that "debt relief excuses and does nothing to reduce corruption."

What if your opponent's speech was disorganized?

We've discussed how to organize refutation on the assumption that your opponent's points were well-organized. Unfortunately, not every-one's speech will have a clear structure. Sometimes you won't be able to tell when one point ends and another begins. If so, chances are that your judges are having the same problem. This type of situation makes it more challenging to organize your clash effectively.

Although you could simply conduct your refutation in an equal-ly scattered way, you would only be dragging yourself down in the process. How do you deal with a disorganized speech? Organize it yourself! As odd as this technique may sound, it will make you more organized and will make it easier for the judges to follow the round. You aren't really assisting your opponent, as you would get credit for improving the quality of the debate. The way to accomplish this task is to read through your notes, find logical breaks, and number the points yourself. For example, you could say, "The first area that our opponent focused on was ... then, the second issue she moved to was ... finally, she discussed a third point ..."

> **Success Tip!**
>
> If your opponent's speech is disorganized, organize it yourself.

CLASH INSURANCE: THE 'SNOWBALL' SYSTEM

Usually, a single argument is met with a single point of refutation. This tactic is typically clear-cut, as it creates a well-matched 'point and counter-point' structure to your refutation. It allows you to be thorough, because you can zero-in on a particular problem and explain your point of contention fully.

Unfortunately, your whole clash against the argument in question relies on this one line of attack. If a judge doesn't buy into your claim, the point will stand. How do you 'insure' yourself against this possibility? You could use multiple angles of attack in sequence, creating a 'snowball' that gathers strength as it moves through an argument. You're creating more reasons to reject the point, even if the judges don't agree fully with every one of them.

Let's take a debate over environmental laws. The Affirmative makes a passionate plea to curb global warming using a combination of regulation and enforcement, aiming to curb carbon dioxide emissions. To illustrate how the Negative could use cumulative, 'snowball' refutation, here's an exaggerated example:

• "Firstly, despite what's often stated in the media, there's no definitive proof that there even is a long-term global warming trend. Scientists around the world are divided on this question—there's no clear consensus. For example, we know that ..."

• "Secondly, *even if* you believe that global warming exists, it can't be firmly established that carbon dioxide is the primary cause. Solar activity—the sun burning hotter in some years than in others—is another possible cause, supported by research from …"

• "Thirdly, *even if* carbon dioxide is a problem, many scientists believe that less than 5% of it is caused by human activity. The rest is naturally occurring, which means that …"

• "Fourthly, *even if* we assume that human activity is a leading cause of carbon dioxide in the atmosphere, are the potential consequences so severe that drastic action is needed? Despite the doomsday scenarios presented by the Affirmative, there's good reason to believe that …"

• "Finally, *even if* significant consequences will result, the Affirmative's proposals aren't the best ways to deal with them because the costs clearly outweigh the benefits. As with historical climate changes, humankind may actually need to adapt to the situation by …"

THE CLINCHER: PLAY TO WIN IN THE REBUTTAL

Over the four constructive speeches, many arguments and counter-arguments have been hurled back and forth. In a typical debate, this could add up to 10 arguments between the two teams, plus refutation of these points. That's a whopping 20 parcels of information that the judges have to process!

Can you blame the judges if they're having trouble deciding who's up and who's down? For this reason, close debates are won and lost in the rebuttal. It's your last chance to make an impression on the judges, which is why your rebuttal strategy is critical to how your side is evaluated. Like closing arguments in a court trial, the rebuttal makes it clear for everyone concerned what has happened in the debate and why your side has prevailed. Let's begin by revisiting the three key roles discussed in Chapter 6:

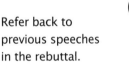

Success Tip!

Refer back to previous speeches in the rebuttal.

• **Refute** the other team's case as a whole.
• **Compare** and contrast the competing themes.
• **Summarize** your team's case.

While you could order your rebuttal based on these three sections, feel free to experiment with what works best for you. The organization of a rebuttal speech is less rigid than that of a constructive speech. You may decide to focus on contrasting the two perspectives, incorporating overall refutation and overall summary into this comparison. Alternatively, you may want to start by analyzing and evaluating the debate chronologically and highlighting the key points made by both sides. It all depends on your personal style and on what you're trying to accomplish with your rebuttal.

It's critical that you understand the difference between clash in a constructive speech and refutation in a rebuttal speech. In first part of the debate, you should have clashed with every important point made by your rival, trying to weaken its case one piece at a time. In a rebuttal speech, your goal is to refute the other team's overall case. A rebuttal speaker shouldn't put much emphasis on detailed analysis of evidence or on taking apart individual arguments.

Watch Out!

Avoid point by point clash in the rebuttal.

The only possible exception to these guidelines is if the second Negative speaker has presented new points, and the rebuttal speech is your team's first chance to respond. If you decide to clash with these arguments individually rather than rolling them into the overall attack, keep the clash brief and put it at the beginning of your rebuttal. Leave the bulk of your rebuttal for overall refutation and summary.

The top rebuttals accomplish one task extremely well: framing the debate. This means putting forth your version of what the debate is actually about—what the judges should consider when making a decision. There are three steps involved in framing the debate, which can also be used as a structure for your rebuttal:

Success Tip!

Use the rebuttal to frame the decision criteria.

Step #1: Tell the judges what the key issues are. Tell them bluntly and concisely—don't skate around them in a roundabout way. You're best off listing and numbering your version of the deciding issues for your judges. This helps them remember your interpretation of the key issues and encourages them to write them down. As with arguments in a constructive speech, you're well-advised not to identify more than two or three issues. Any more will be too much for you to talk about and for your judges to digest in such a short speech.

Step #2: Explain why they're the key issues. A judge can be forgiven for thinking, "On what basis have you selected *those* issues as the *deciding* issues?" If you're going to condense the debate down to core themes or zero-in on selected arguments, it's your responsibility to justify your decision. Tell the judges why the entire debate rests on the pillars you've identified.

Step #3: Argue how you've come out ahead on these issues. Of course, it only makes sense to choose issues that you feel fall clearly on your side of the resolution. Drive home these advantages in your rebuttal. Explain how you've prevailed on these dimensions and why that means you've won the debate.

If you're delivering the Negative rebuttal, one effective way to frame the debate around your key issues is to tell the Affirmative what exactly it must do in its rebuttal. This tactic can throw off your opponent's rebuttal, as well as encourage your judges to pay attention to how well your rival responds to your challenges. But only include those issues that you're very confident fall clearly on your side of the debate. There's nothing worse than laying out what you feel should be the key decision criteria, only to have the Affirmative team prove itself right on each of the points.

For example, you could say, "So what are the two core issues of this debate? What must the first Affirmative speaker prove to you in her rebuttal? Firstly, she must show you why a tax dedicated to roads won't end up in the government's general coffers and in other departments. We've revealed how easy it is for this to happen. Secondly, she must show you that …"

How should you respond if you're the Affirmative rebuttal speaker and this tactic is used against you? There are two options: tackle the issues directly, or ignore them altogether. The first option is risky, because you're allowing the Negative to control your speech. If you're very confident that you can explain why you won on the criteria presented, by all means go ahead and do so. But if you fall short, you're bound to lose the debate. The second option allows you to carry out the rebuttal as you see fit. If you're going to ignore the Negative's criteria, you have to explain clearly why they're not the key issues of the debate. Logically, it then falls on you to provide a different version of the key issues and to justify why your interpretation is right.

This chapter is perhaps one of the most important in the book, because it told you about a key aspect of a vibrant debate: the point by point and overall refutation of the other team's arguments. If you want to excel at debate, it's essential that you understand the different ways to make counter-arguments and how to deliver a rebuttal speech.

Chapter 8: Keys to Success

✔ **Clash with every argument**. Leaving a point unchallenged suggests that you agree with it and makes your opponent's case stronger. Refutation may be a challenging, 'on the spot' skill, but it's essential to the debate.

✔ **Think about the different ways to refute a point**. Analyze whether the argument is logical and rests on sound assumptions. Look for contradictory, irrelevant, or poorly linked points.

✔ **Simplify your refutation with labels**. Label each of your opponent's points in a way that communicates what you think is wrong with them. This tactic makes is easier to discuss the core themes, rather than having to describe each point in detail.

✔ **Be organized when you clash**. For each point, say what you're refuting, refute it, and explain why it matters. Using your flow sheet as an aid, work methodically (usually in order) through your opponent's points. Place greater emphasis on the most important arguments.

✔ **In the rebuttal, focus on 'big picture' ideas**. Frame the debate in a way that favors your side of the resolution. Tell the judges what the key issues are, why they're the key issues, and how you've won on these issues. Rather than engaging in point by point clash, focus on the debate's key themes.

CHAPTER 9
On That Point:
Navigating Parliamentary Debate

Coming Up!

In this section, you'll learn about the procedures and techniques of parliamentary debate. You'll discover how to use questions, or Points of Information, to damage an opponent's case, and how to react when questions are fired at you.

THE PARLIAMENTARY TRADITION

Parliamentary debate has a long history in legislatures around the world. The United States Congress, the British House of Commons, and the German Bundestag are all examples of national legislatures. In these chambers, the great debates of society take place. Elected representatives from various regions gather to debate laws on economic, social, and foreign affairs. The debates tend to be lively and vigorous, even becoming public spectacles at their most heated moments.

> **Did You Know?**
>
> Modern parliamentary debate started in England.

Many of the features seen in national parliaments have worked their way into student parliamentary debating, such as the titles of the participants and other formalities. The student version shrinks the number of debaters from several hundred to four, in most styles. As with real parliaments, there is a Government and an Opposition.

The key feature of this style is your ability to ask questions, known as Points of Information, while your opponent is speaking. You can also heckle when someone else has the floor, making for some humorous and spontaneous moments. (It's less raucous, though, than the barrage of simultaneous heckles commonly seen in actual legislatures.) Other than these elements, the skills discussed in previous chapters apply to parliamentary style as well.

LEARNING THE LINGO

One of the first features you'll notice about parliamentary debate is the difference in language compared to other forms of debate. Like functioning legislatures, parliamentary style has its own lingo. Making mistakes relating to appropriate language won't weaken your case. But it's important to use the right terms, because doing so shows that you're familiar with how the style works. Here are some of the basic parliamentary debate terms that you should get to know:

The Speaker is to parliamentary debate what the Chairperson is to other styles of competition. The proper way to refer to this person is "Mr. Speaker" or "Madame Speaker." As in real legislatures, the Speaker has the final authority over rules and procedures. Everything you say flows through the Speaker. For example, "Madame Speaker, today we will show you why gambling should be banned."

The Government is essentially the Affirmative team—the side that supports the motion. Rather than a first Affirmative speaker and a second Affirmative speaker, there is a Prime Minister (P.M.) and a Minister of the Crown (M.C.), respectively. These positions don't imply rank or authority within a team. They're used simply to identify roles.

The Opposition, sometimes called Her Majesty's Loyal Opposition, is like the Negative team in that it argues against the motion. Unlike the titles first speaker and second speaker used in other styles, the team members are called the Member of the Opposition (M.O.) and the Leader of the Opposition (L.O.).

The Bill is another term for the resolution. In addition to resolutions and motions, parliaments also pass Bills. A Bill usually refers to a policy. However, the term used to describe the topic will vary with different versions of parliamentary style.

The House is the chamber in which the debate takes place. You'll hear phrases like, "This House is now adjourned" or "We've made three points before this House today."

The Honorable Members are the debaters arguing for or against the issue. This phrase is commonly used as a respectful way to address the opposing team's debaters. If addressing everyone in the room, it's a more fitting alternative to the less formal "ladies and gentlemen."

To provide you with a clear understanding of what parliamentary language seems like, here's an example of a passage from academic style debate 'translated' into the parliamentary lexicon:

• *Academic style debate*: "Mr. Chairperson, the Negative told this round of debate that the resolution must fall because of what it claims is an inconsistency in the first Affirmative speaker's arguments."

• *Parliamentary style debate*: "Mr. Speaker, the Opposition told this House to vote against this Bill because of what the Honorable Member claims is an inconsistency in the Prime Minister's arguments."

PARLIAMENTARY SHAPE AND STRUCTURE

Like the style of debate discussed in previous chapters, there's no common shape and structure for parliamentary debate. Depending on where you are, what level you're at, and what tournament you're debating in, the times and roles will vary. Here's a basic structure that applies, in a general sense, to most parliamentary styles of debate:

Prime Minister (P.M.)	5 minutes
Member of the Opposition (M.O.)	8 minutes
Minister of the Crown (M.C.)	8 minutes
Leader of the Opposition (L.O.)	8 minutes
Prime Minister (P.M.)	3 minutes

Although everyone has the same amount of speaking time, you'll notice that the Prime Minister's time is split. The first speech is a constructive speech, and the second speech is a rebuttal speech. Also, the first five minutes of the Leader of the Opposition's speech is the constructive portion, and the last three minutes is the rebuttal portion. There's no clear break, though, between these two parts. The roles of each speaker are generally comparable to the Affirmative and Negative roles outlined in Chapter 6:

Prime Minister
• *Define* the terms of the resolution.
• *Present* the Government's case, including specific arguments.

Member of the Opposition
• *Clash* with the Prime Minister's arguments.
• *Present* the Opposition's case, including specific arguments.

Minister of the Crown
• *Clash* with the Member of the Opposition's arguments.
• *Continue* the Government's case with new arguments.
• *Defend* the Prime Minister's arguments, if necessary.

Leader of the Opposition
• *Clash* with the Minister of the Crown's arguments.
• *Continue* the Opposition's case with new arguments.
• *Defend* the Member of the Opposition's arguments, if necessary.

- *Refute* the Government's case as a whole.
- *Summarize* the Opposition's case as a whole.

Prime Minister
- *Clash* with the Leader of the Opposition's arguments, if necessary.
- *Refute* the Opposition's case as a whole.
- *Summarize* the Government's case as whole.

WHAT'S THE POINT OF A POINT?

Simply put, Points of Information are your opportunity to ask tough question to your opponent during his or her constructive speech (they're not allowed in rebuttals). Points of Information take your competitors off their game plan, forcing them to respond to your challenge. To ask a question, stand up during your rival's speech and say, "Point of Information" or "On that point." Your opponent may either allow you to ask your question or signal you to sit down. Ask questions with one or more of the following goals in mind:

Dispute the member's argument. This purpose is the most common use of a Point of Information. If you believe that your opponent's point is either flawed or illogical, ask a question that forces the issue. For example, "If a judge is supposed to interpret the law without regard to what's popular, wouldn't electing judges essentially force them to cater to the whims of public opinion?" Even if the debater finds a way to defend the point, at minimum you've planted seeds of doubt into the minds of your judges.

Contest the evidence presented. A word of caution: don't waste your Point of Information on an evidence dispute unless it will inflict serious damage to your opponent's case. If used carefully, disputing evidence can weaken a key foundation of the other team's case or hurt its credibility on the issue. For example, "How can you use the 2000 economic data to argue that 11% unemployment is a serious problem, when the 2005 report from the same source indicated that the rate had dropped to 7%?" You would certainly have them on the ropes with that one.

Suggest the point's irrelevance. A great way to oppose a point without countering it directly is to challenge how closely it fits with the issue at hand. If asked at the end of an argument, your question can throw off your opponent. For example, "Okay, so you've told us how an American drug company can distribute this medicine in Africa, but how is that even relevant if you've specified that the case is about funding arrangements *between governments?*" Well, there goes the past minute of your opponent's speech.

Introduce an upcoming argument. It's always nice if you can combine a question on an argument that the member has just made with a hint of what's to come in your speech. Doing so alerts the judges to what you're going to say, shifting the focus of the debate closer to your team. For example, "If we were to follow your plan and end the space shuttle program, wouldn't we also be cutting off the scientific and medical experiments that have proven so valuable in the recent years?" If delivered during the Prime Minister's speech, this point would get you into the debate early.

Provide a reminder of a past argument. It's easy for your points to be forgotten, especially if they're introduced early in the debate. Bringing up one of your previous points in a question on your opponent's argument reinforces your case. For example, "But we've already shown that standardized exams encourage schools to improve their performance compared to others schools. If, as you now suggest, we simply stop making the results public, wouldn't it defeat this very valuable motivational purpose?" This question counters your opponent's new argument while reintroducing a past argument.

Clarify a confusing definition. Only ask for an explanation if what your opponent said is both unclear to everyone and is critical to the debate. Otherwise, save your opportunity for a more significant question. If, however, you use this type of Point of Information wisely, it can win you points by clarifying the debate for your team and for the judges. For example, "Just to be clear, when you talk about banning 'the violent sport of boxing', are you referring only to professional competition or also to Olympic competition, which involves helmets and softer gloves?" This way, everyone will be debating the same issue.

Point out a contradiction. Catching an inconsistency on the spot can be a great way to discredit an argument. This is true both for consistency within a speech and between partners. For example, "Okay, so you're saying that the government should fund theatres because they're so popular, but your partner said that the case for subsidies is that most theatres don't sell enough tickets to stay afloat on their own. Which one is it?" Placing a 'wedge' between partners can steal your opponent's thunder in the middle of its speeches.

RISE AT THE RIGHT TIME

You've got a question that you're itching to ask. When do you jump off your chair to ask it? There are two factors you should consider. Firstly, when it will have the most impact, and secondly, when the speaker is most likely to accept it. Timing is more important than most debaters will appreciate. A well-timed question helps you seize

Success Tip!
Think carefully about the timing of your questions.

the agenda and take control the debate. On the other hand, poor timing makes your question seem out of place—a distraction to the debate. The following are good places to ask a Point of Information:

After a key part of a constructive point. Each main argument usually consists of a number of explanations that help form the point. Rising after one of these explanations may be to your advantage, since a tough question can throw off the flow of the argument. If the speaker rejects your point, you may have an opportunity to persist at least one more time before he or she moves to an entirely new argument.

At the end of a complete argument. Rising at the end of an argument allows you to damage the entire point at once. It gives you time to take in all of explanations and evidence used to support the argument. Listen very carefully for what appears to be the speaker's concluding sentence to the point in question. The speaker is most likely to accept your Point of Information when the argument is complete, since he or she will feel confident that the argument has been justified fully.

In response to damaging refutation. Let's face it, sometimes your opponent will make a great counter-argument to what you thought was a bullet-proof point. Rather than accepting it lying down, show that you're confident by rising on a Point of Information. This will give you an opportunity to challenge refutation that would otherwise inflict serious damage to your case. Even if your question isn't accepted, at least you'll be making it clear to your judges that you have something to say about your opponent's refutation.

WHEN TO STAY PUT

Unfortunately, even seasoned debaters are tempted to ask questions when the timing isn't right. The question may be brilliant, but the effect is seriously weakened because of poor timing. It's important to understand why asking questions at other times isn't a good idea:

During the introduction. In most parliamentary debates, the first minute of a speech is 'protected time'. This means that it's against the rules to rise on a Point of Information. Even if it's allowed, you accomplish little by rising on a Point of Information when your opponent has just introduced the case theme. How can you challenge a case that hasn't yet been developed?

During the conclusion. Since a Point of Information is meant as a targeted challenge of a particular argument, asking a question when the debater is talking about broader themes is poor timing. Note that the last minute of someone's speech, like the first minute, is protected time in most parliamentary debates.

Immediately after an argument is introduced. It's best to wait until your opponent has developed at least part of an argument before you jump all over it. The answer will probably be some variation of "Well, thank you for the question. I was just about to get into that."

In the middle of a sentence. It may be tempting to throw off the member in the middle of a statement, but doing so makes it seem that you're intentionally interrupting your opponent. Also, you could miss an important part of the argument if you rise prematurely.

When the debate has moved on. Sure, you may have a burning question to ask concerning your opponent's previous point. But once the debate has moved to the next argument, it's too late. Your question will seem out of place.

If you've been rejected several times. There's nothing wrong with persisting a couple of times when you have something important to ask. But if you're told to sit down repeatedly over a short period of time, the member is making it very clear that your point will not be accepted. Continuing to rise will make it seem like you're needlessly interrupting your opponent's speech.

STANDING UP TO STAND OUT

When you stand up hoping to ask a Point of Information, the focus of the debate momentarily turns to you. It's important that you have a good 'stage presence' when you do so. Below are some tips that will help you make a strong impression when you rise to ask a question:

Success Tip!

Make sure that both you and your partner ask questions.

State your request in a simple way. Some debaters prefer to foreshadow questions which phrases like "On democracy" or "On rationality." While appropriate if used occasionally, it certainly isn't necessary. The best ways to request an opportunity to ask a question are saying "Point of Information" or "On that point." Trying to make a full argument is pushing it too far. For example, saying "On the need to punish people who pose no harm to society" makes it look like you're trying to deliver part of your speech during your opponent's speech.

Stand up quickly and confidently. If you're going to rise on a Point of Information, be decisive about it. Rising slowly or in a hesitant way conveys uncertainty to your judges.

Address the member by name. We're naturally more receptive to other people when we're called by our names. Saying "On that point, Greg" or "Point of Information, Ms. Jones" can be a subtle way to increase the chances of your Point of Information being accepted.

Stand up one person at a time. There's no use in standing up with your partner, as it's needlessly distracting. It may even look like you're trying to compete with your partner for attention.

FIELDING THE BARRAGE OF QUESTIONS

While you may prefer to speak without interruption, it's inevitable that your opponents will rise to ask Points of Information. Although it's important to show that you're capable of defending your arguments, you don't want to let the questions get you off track either. Here are some tips to help you manage Points of Information:

Accept two Points of Information. If you accept one question, you're at least showing a willingness to face criticism. But especially during an eight minute constructive speech, it could still seem like you're trying to minimize challenges. Accepting two points is the norm. Allowing more than two questions gives your opponents too much control over your speech.

Watch Out!

Don't let Points of Information control your speech.

Allow reasonable time for the question. If you've accepted a point, it's usually inappropriate to cut off your opponent before the question has been asked fully. The exception is if the questioner is rambling excessively, taking up more than 10 to 15 seconds of your valuable time. In this scenario, be polite but firm in order to regain control of your speech. For example, you could say, "Thank you, I understand what you're getting at."

Answer the question completely. Some debaters will shrug off a question as irrelevant or weak, without actually answering it. This may suggest that you're unwilling or unable to defend your argument. Always provide a clear and decisive answer to a Point of Information.

Transition back to your speech quickly. It shouldn't take you more than a couple of sentences to answer a question. Going on for longer allows the question to dictate your speech. Once you've answered the question, make a smooth transition to stay on track. For example, you could say, "Coming back to my second point ..." or "I'd now like to move on to my third argument."

Success Tip!

Keep your answers short and move on.

DON'T HECKLE FOR THE HECK OF IT

Heckling can be an interesting, spontaneous, and humorous part of parliamentary debate. Unfortunately, it's also the most misused. A heckle is a short and witty comment that gets to the point in a few words, usually five or less. It's not your opportunity to hear yourself talk. It's not your opportunity to continue your speech during your opponent's speech. Since heckling is more often used poorly than well, perhaps it's appropriate to focus on weak ways to heckle:

Shouting "shame, shame" or "that's wrong." You'll have your chance to plead your case when you speak. This type of heckling is a rude interruption, as tempting as it might seem.

Demanding "proof" or "source." It's up to the member to present the evidence how he or she sees fit. The judges will decide whether the opposing team has supported its arguments well. Heckling in this way makes you seem petty.

Asking questions. If your Point of Information is rejected, it doesn't give you a license to get it through the 'back door' by heckling. A heckle isn't meant to start a back and forth dialogue.

Making arguments. Refutation should go in your speech, not your opponent's speech. Trying to argue over the voice of your rival is ineffective at best, and disrespectful at worst.

Heckling repeatedly. Undoubtedly, the occasional good heckle can lighten up the debate. Doing so over and over again, though, interrupts the flow of debate excessively and may cause the judges to deduct points from your individual score.

HOW TO HANDLE HECKLING

There is one, simple rule for responding to heckling: don't respond to heckling. Never start a 'side debate' with your opponent during your valuable speaking time. Responding to heckling serves to legitimize or give undue attention to your rival. Simply ignore it, and move on as you normally would have. Even looking at your opponent while he or she is heckling diverts attention away from you.

RULINGS ON THE RULES: POINTS OF ORDER

Parliamentary debate has countless rules that participants are supposed to follow. In real parliaments, there are thick books describing all of these rules in detail. You're not supposed to put your hands in your pockets (you could be hiding a weapon), nor are you allowed to have a pen in your hand (that could be viewed as a weapon). Debaters aren't supposed to cross onto the other team's side of the floor, and standing in a place that obstructs the Speaker's view of any of the parliamentarians is a big taboo. And the list goes on.

If you want to accuse your opponent of a rule violation, you would rise and say, "Mr. Speaker, I rise on a Point of Order" or, more simply, "Point of Order." At this juncture, the person who has the floor must sit down while the Speaker decides "Point well taken" if in agreement or "Point not well taken" if in disagreement.

Should you follow all of the time-honored rules of parliamentary procedure? Yes. But should you demand enforcement if another debater doesn't? Probably not. You may think that doing so makes you seem sophisticated and intelligent. But at the same, you'll be interrupting the flow of debate for frivolous reasons. Most judges won't be impressed. Only raise a Point of Order for the most serious of violations. This will probably never happen, but it's helpful to know about this feature of parliamentary debate in case it comes up.

> **Watch Out!**
>
> Don't raise frivolous Points of Order or Personal Privilege.

NO OFFENSE: POINTS OF PERSONAL PRIVILEGE

In addition to following parliamentary rules, debaters are expected to speak honestly and respectfully. One reason to raise a Point of Personal Privilege is if a member of the opposing team makes a personally offensive remark. Another cause is if your opponent seriously misquotes you. The process is similar to a Point of Order. You say, "Mr. Speaker, I rise on a Point of Personal Privilege" and the Speaker rules, "Point well taken" or "Point not well taken."

While it's useful to be aware of this feature, you should rarely, if ever, have to use it. Surely, if you're about to break into tears because your opponent made a vulgar remark, you could decide to raise an objection. A blatant misquotation that could seriously harm your case might be another exception. Hopefully, none of these instances will come up. In any case, it will probably be quite clear to the judges if someone is being rude or is misrepresenting your case. Let your opponent's behavior speak for itself.

By following the basic guidelines presented in this chapter, you'll be well on your way to navigating a parliamentary debate. This style can be lively and interesting, and how you use these techniques will play a significant role in how well you do.

Chapter 9: Keys to Success

✔ **Ask challenging, well-timed Points of Information**. A strong question on an argument made immediately beforehand is a great way to counter your opponent's case. You'll also force your opponent to go on the defensive.

✔ **Answer Points of Information directly and move on**. Don't let a question get you off track. Be concise in your response and transition back to your speech quickly. It's essential that you maintain control over your speech.

✔ **Keep heckles short, witty, and to the point**. Heckles aren't meant for you to make arguments or to ask questions. They're usually humorous, spur of the moment jibes. If you aren't sure you can do it well, remember that heckling isn't a requirement.

✔ **Follow the conventions of parliamentary debate**. In particular, make sure to address the Speaker and your opponents correctly. You should also follow specific rules, such as not holding a pen in your hand (it's poor form in any style). However, don't rise on a Point of Order for this type of petty rule violation.

CHAPTER 10

Yes or No:
Commanding the Cross-Examination

Coming Up!

In a cross-examination debate, a period of questioning by a member of the opposing team follows each constructive speech. This chapter will show you how to ask a series of tough questions when you're the cross-examiner. It will also show you how to stand your ground when you're the one under fire.

SAVVY ON THE SPOT

A cross-examination is a lively, 'heat of the moment' opportunity for you to show your command of the debate. After each of the first four speeches, a member of the other team has a few minutes to cross-examine the speaker. Put another way, it's your opportunity to pepper your opponent with a barrage of questions intended to weaken his or her arguments. If you're the one being cross-examined, it's your chance to show that you're confident in your arguments and that you can withstand sustained criticism.

At the end of a constructive speech, the speaker will make a statement like, "I now stand open for cross-examination." The cross-examiner then rises and begins the questioning. Different versions of cross-examination debate have slightly different structures. Here's a typical example of a speaker and cross-examiner configuration:

1st Affirmative Constructive (1AC):	6 minutes
Cross-examination by 2nd Negative:	4 minutes
1st Negative Constructive (1NC):	6 minutes
Cross-examination by 1st Affirmative:	4 minutes
2nd Affirmative Constructive (2AC):	6 minutes
Cross-examination by 1st Negative:	4 minutes
2nd Negative Constructive (2NC):	6 minutes
Cross-examination by 2nd Affirmative:	4 minutes
1st Negative Rebuttal (1NR):	4 minutes
1st Affirmative Rebuttal (1AR):	4 minutes

CHIPPING AWAY: CROSS-EXAMINER GOALS

If you're the one asking the questions, you should go into the cross-examination with specific objectives in mind. It's your golden opportunity to chip away at your opponent's case. But if you don't know what you're trying to accomplish, you'll be stuck firing off unfocused, unrelated questions that don't significantly damage your opponent's case. What are some of the goals you should be trying to accomplish?

Expose Errors. If your opponent has made statements that are either contradictory or inaccurate, the cross-examination period is a great place to point them out. It can be even more effective than doing so in your own speech, because the judges will see your opponent struggling to defend the errors.

Attain Admissions. Forcing your opponent to admit a fact or point that you believe is important to the issue at hand can leave you a step ahead at the end of the cross-examination period. The speaker will appear to be retreating as you draw out admissions that are helpful to your side of the debate.

Attack Arguments. As with refutation, a cross-examination is an opportunity to challenge the logic behind the other team's points. The advantage of a cross-examination is that you can craft a line of questioning in a way that gradually and systematically weakens your opponent's argument. This leaves it 'exposed' for further refutation later on in the debate.

Setup Points. A cross-examination isn't intended for you to present new arguments. However, you may find it useful to establish the *foundation* for a future point without completely giving it away. One such use is establishing the validity of an assumption necessary for one of your upcoming arguments.

Clear Up Confusion. If your opponent has presented definitions or arguments that are confusing, spending a short period of time to bring clarity may be valuable. You'll get the credit not only for showing that your opponent was unclear, but also for making it easier for the judges to understand what's happening in the debate.

TOUGH AND TIGHT QUESTIONS

The type of question you ask has a significant influence on the type of answer you'll receive, even if the intent is exactly the same. It's important that you to understand how to phrase a question in order to achieve your objective. Questions can be grouped into three categories: open-ended, semi-directed, and leading.

Open-Ended Questions

Open-ended questions invite and encourage the responder to provide lengthy, drawn out answers. When used in a cross-examination, they allow the speaker to take up time elaborating and explaining, which isn't to your advantage as a cross-examiner. Rather than enabling you to drive toward a specific objective, they allow your opponent to control the cross-examination. For example, "How severe do you think the problem of speeding is in this city?"

Semi-Directed Questions

Semi-directed questions suggest what the response should include. They sometimes call for a particular fact to be stated. Although more effective than open-ended questions, they don't drive at your point quickly enough, especially if the speaker doesn't know the answer or tries to maneuver into a related area. For example, "Are you aware of what the latest police report said concerning the number of people killed in this city last year because of speeding drivers?" (This question only encourages an answer such as, "No, please enlighten me.")

Leading Questions

Leading questions imply an answer to which you want the responder to agree. Therefore, they serve to make an argument while pushing for an admission. These are the types of questions you want to be asking most often in a cross-examination, because they allow you to control the process and drive toward an end goal. For example, "Would you not agree that the 1,442 deaths and 10,662 injuries caused in this city last year by speeding drivers show very clearly that this is a severe public safety problem?"

> **Success Tip!**
>
> Keep your questions short, simple, and to the point.

GIVING YOUR RIVAL A GRILLING

We've seen why knowing your objective helps you focus your cross-examination, and we've covered the different types of questions. It's now time to discuss how specifically to go about reaching your goals.

The key to successful cross-examining is asking direct, targeted questions in a series. Firing off random questions on a wide variety of issues will leave you without any key takeaways at the end. Here are some smart strategies for successful cross-examining:

Ask one question at a time. Multipart questions show a lack of flow and focus. You're also required to allow the speaker enough time to answer all of your questions, which makes it harder for you to regain control when you want to move on. A single question is more focused, as it helps you drill down a specific point. It's best to follow up with another question once you've received an answer.

Avoid sarcasm or mockery. There's nothing worse than looking like you're trying to 'beat up' on your opponent. Stick to intelligent, purposeful questions that show confidence and command of the debate. If you have your opponent on the defensive, sounding arrogant about it paints you in a negative light.

Ask leading, "yes or no" questions. Your goal in a cross-examination is to force a quick, anticipated response from the speaker. Ideally, you want your opponent to say "yes" or "no" without leaving much room for a lengthy explanation.

Permit a brief qualification. Even if you ask a "yes or no" question, the speaker has a right to qualify his or her answer. If, however, your opponent starts rambling, you're well within your rights to cut off the answer promptly and respectfully.

Keep your questions brief and to the point. Lengthy introductory explanations make it look more like a speech and less like a cross-examination. Granted, you're trying to argue your perspective in a cross-examination. But let your questions suggest your line of argumentation, rather than trying to make arguments directly.

> **Watch Out!**
>
> Don't start 'speech-making' in your cross-examination.

Plan a series of questions. On a given issue, prepare to ask at least six to eight questions to get to the point or admission that you're seeking. This tactic will provide key areas of focus for the cross-examination, leaving the judges with the sense that you've inflicted damage to specific arguments. Simply scratching the surface of many arguments leaves everyone wondering what, if anything, was accomplished.

Persist in response to indecisiveness. If the speaker tries to avoid a question deliberately, ask it again in different words and with a firmer tone. Don't let your opponent get away with being inconclusive. In most case, evasiveness suggests there's something to hide. Be determined to get a direct answer to your question.

Know when to move on. When you get to the end of a questioning sequence, your opponent will be very reluctant to admit what you want in order to avoid making a damaging remark. Once the cross-examination is at a deadlock, move on to another line of questioning or conclude. There's nothing worse than going hopelessly back and forth on the same question when both sides have clearly staked out their respective positions.

Maintain control of the questioning. Sometimes the speaker will try to turn around the cross-examination by asking questions back to you. This is a trick aimed at shifting the power away from you. Don't let it happen. If your opponent starts asking questions, remind him or her that it's your cross-examination.

FAULTY TO FANTASTIC: SAMPLE QUESTIONS

Now that you know the tools of the trade for asking powerful cross-examination questions, let's take a look at a few examples of questions to see what makes (and breaks) a cross-examination. Notice how each question progresses from a poor wording to a good wording. Knowing the difference between weak and strong questions will greatly improve your cross-examination.

Internet Censorship (Open-Ended to Leading)

• *Poor Question*: "What do you think about how easy or difficult it is to verify the age of each person who wants to enter an adult website?"

• *Okay Question*: "Isn't it challenging to check the age of someone entering an Internet site, since there's no face to face contact?"

• *Good Question:* "Would you not agree that the unrestricted nature of Internet search makes it almost impossible to verify the age of someone entering a site?"

Food Labeling (Speechmaking to Brief)

• *Poor Question:* "There are many people who don't want to eat genetically-modified foods. We believe they deserve the right to know if a particular item at the grocery store has been genetically-modified in any way. Required labeling of genetically-modified products would help them make the choices they desire. Don't you agree?"

• *Okay Question:* "Considering that many people don't want to buy any genetically-modified foods and that labeling is the only way to allow them to make informed choices, do you agree that mandatory labeling would protect a consumer's right to know what's in a food product?"

• *Good Question:* "Would you acknowledge that many consumers prefer not to eat genetically-modified foods?"

Commercialization of Sport (Multipart to Single)

• *Poor Question:* "Wouldn't you agree that corporate sponsorship injects more money into sport programs, which helps train athletes and leads to stronger performance at the Olympics and other competitions?"

• *Okay Question:* "Do you acknowledge that sports facilities use sponsorship money to stay afloat and to train athletes?"

• *Good Question:* "Do you agree that many training facilities receive a significant portion of their revenues from corporate sponsorships?"

Joint Peacekeeping (Mocking to Intelligent)

• *Poor Question:* "Wouldn't you agree that your grandiose plan to have rivals work together is a bit like asking kids to be part of the same group project after they've had a big fight?"

• *Okay Question:* "Do you agree that asking enemies to be friends all of a sudden is really a teamwork disaster waiting to happen?"

• *Good Question*: "Do you agree that countries work together more effectively if they have a long history of friendly relations?"

PLANNING THE PROCESS

Like any speech, a cross-examination must have structure in order to be effective. Usually, you have three to four minutes to cross-examine the speaker. This length of time allows you to cover more than one issue. One effective technique is 'signposting' your cross-examination. For example, you could say, "The first area I want to ask you about is the legal aspect of professional boxing." Once you've completed this line of questioning, you could state, "Now that I've challenged your points about legality, let's move on to your assumptions concerning moral hazards." The advantage of breaking down the cross-examination is that the judges will grasp more easily the distinct themes that you've covered.

> **Success Tip!**
>
> Plan a full line of questioning with an end goal.

STANDING YOUR GROUND: SPEAKER GOALS

Of course, the questioner has an opportunity to go on the offensive during the cross-examination period. But as the speaker being cross-examined, you can do much more than simply weather the storm. Instead, you can strive to come out of the cross-examination appearing even stronger than before it. As the speaker, there are a number of objectives you may want to accomplish:

Pre-refute refutation. Your cross-examiner is trying to expose flaws that will assist him or her in future clash against your arguments. If you can deflect and debunk the attacks during the cross-examination, you're essentially negating what the other team plans to use as its refutation. Done effectively, this tactic can leave your opponent scrambling to find another angle of attack.

Stifle the questioner. Your opponent will likely have a series of questions to ask you on a given issue. In most cases, he or she has anticipated what you'll say about the preliminary questions in order to setup the more damaging ones. If you can sidetrack the cross-examiner early on by presenting fair but unexpected answers, you can leave your opponent struggling to get back on track. In addition, you'll force your rival to take up valuable cross-examination time scurrying to get to the point of contention.

Defend your case. If you can stand tough against a strong cross-examiner, you'll have gone a long way in showing confidence in your case. The judges will view bold and intelligent responses to tough questions very favorably. They show that you can face criticism on the spot, which emphasizes the strength of your arguments.

> **Success Tip!**
>
> Anticipate the cross-examiner's next questions.

YES, NO, MAYBE SO: ANSWERING QUESTIONS

The best cross-examiners will try to force you into to simple, "yes or no" answers. Remember that your cross-examiner has likely planned out a series of questions aimed at extracting an admission from you. Here are some of the keys to answering questions effectively:

Qualify your answers. Your cross-examiner is hoping you'll answer a simple "yes" or "no" so that he or she can quickly move on with the line of questioning. Don't let your cross-examiner dominate you in this way. There are usually nuances, exceptions, and details that will strengthen your answer. Providing an explanation to your answer will help stifle the cross-examiner and show your confidence.

Be concise. The risk of qualifying your answers is that you'll start to ramble. Going too far with explanations will result in you losing points. You don't want to be seen as killing time by making speeches instead of providing answers. Do qualify your answers, but get to the point quickly and let the cross-examiner move on.

Refer back to your speech. When relevant to the answer, saying, for example, "As I discussed in my second point ..." or "We've already explained that ..." reminds the judges of what you said previously. It also makes your answers stronger by using the backing of arguments that have already been well-developed.

Don't pass it on to your partner. Saying, for example, "My partner will address your question in her upcoming speech" makes you seem unsure. In addition, you've now made a promise that your partner has to keep, throwing your team's next speech off track. Always provide a complete answer yourself.

Never give in. It doesn't matter if your cross-examiner has you on the ropes with a series of very tough questions. Always defend yourself, even if your opponent has done damage to your case. Conceding a point only worsens the damage, making it next to irreversible.

Look at the audience as well. There's nothing wrong with looking exclusively at your questioner. It certainly makes sense, since he or she is the one with whom you're conversing. However, also making eye contact with the audience makes you seem more engaging and confident in what you're saying.

Don't communicate with your partner. Whispering or gesturing between you and your partner makes it seem like you need a 'clutch' in order to answer the question. It's essential that you seem independently confident in your speech.

Answer questions, don't ask them. Some debaters find it clever to try turning around the cross-examination by asking questions to the cross-examiner. This tactic will be obvious to the judges, who will typically view it as inappropriate. Stick to your role by answering questions asked of you by your opponent.

Be decisive. It isn't good practice to be deliberately vague, as it seems like you're trying to evade your opponent or that you lack confidence. Make sure your answers are clear and direct. Answers such as, "Well, it just depends" or "It's tough to say, really" appear very indecisive.

ADEPT ANSWERS

We've discussed the keys to answering cross-examination questions. Now let's take a look at a few examples. The following sample answers will lead you from a poor response through to a good response:

Unqualified to Explained: "Do you not agree that advertising designed to appeal to our emotions makes us buy things with little benefit?"

• *Poor Answer*: "No, I don't agree."

• *Okay Answer*: "No, because if it satisfies our emotions, then it does indeed have a benefit."

• *Good Answer*: "Not necessarily. We don't get personal satisfaction only from what we 'need'. We also have nonessential 'wants' that advertisers aim to satisfy, such as feeling good about wearing a particular brand of clothing."

Concession to Case Defense: "Is it not true that students would benefit from more music training?"

• *Poor Answer*: "Sure, they would of course get some benefit."

• *Okay Answer*: "They may get a benefit, but there would be significant time and money costs."

• *Good Answer*: "Despite the enhancement, increasing the time spent on music class would take away from other courses. There's limited time, and the trade-off away from core subjects would be harmful."

Indecisive to Confident: "Do you acknowledge that prison amenities and activities make it easier to go from being a criminal to acting as a responsible member of society?"

• *Poor Answer*: "Well, it depends. Everyone is different."

• *Okay Answer*: "Although they perhaps make for an easier transition, they go slightly against the core goals of prisons, namely punishment for crimes and deterrence against future crimes."

• *Good Answer*: "Quite the contrary. Prisons are meant to punish criminals and deter crime. Prison luxuries send the opposite message."

Questioning to Answering: "Isn't it the case that corporate executives are accountable only to the profit demands of shareholders?"

• *Poor Answer*: "But do you not think that they consider how the public will view their actions? Wouldn't you agree that they also want to have a good public image?"

• *Okay Answer*: "For certain, shareholders may be one stakeholder, but you must admit that they consider public perceptions and their own reputations as well."

• *Good Answer*: "No, they have to balance demands for short-term profits with their goal of creating a positive, long-term relationship with the public. Executives know that a strong corporate image will help the company over time."

HAMMER IT HOME: USING THE CROSS-EXAMINATION

Standing alone, strong performance in a cross-examination period can help your team considerably. But can you stretch the effects of a cross-examination into other parts of the debate? Absolutely. Applying the cross-examination to the overall debate highlights and reinforces moments in the cross-examination that you feel benefited your case. This tool applies both to cross-examinations that involved you and those in which your partner was a participant. Additionally, although you'll usually find more material to use from when your team asked the questions, your answers may also be good material for future speeches. Here are some ways to use the cross-examination:

> **Success Tip!**
>
> Remind the judges of the cross-examination.

Highlight a flaw. If your team has exposed weakness in one of your opponent's arguments, remind the judges that you've done so. Since you don't have a full opportunity to analyze and criticize your opponent's answers during a cross-examination, an uninterrupted speech provides you with a valuable chance to explain exactly how the cross-examination exposed the flaws.

Use an admission for refutation. Bringing up concessions made by your opponents during cross-examination periods is a way of turning their own words into refutation. An admission provided in an answer makes your clash significantly stronger, since you don't have to spend very much of your valuable time explaining and proving a point that the other side has already conceded.

Lay the foundation for your argument. Although it's less common than using the cross-examination for refutation, you can use an admission gained during a cross-examination to support the basis of a constructive point. This tool can be used to defend previous points or to lay the foundation for new points. Using cross-examination concessions in this way makes it tougher for the other side to clash, since your opponent appears to be at least in partial agreement.

Reinforce your strengths. An opposing team will try fervently to weaken your arguments while cross-examining you. In many cases, your rival will go in circles without inflicting any harm, helping you show confidence in your case. Referring back to the cross-examination can aid in reinforcing that your points have passed the test of criticism. It's a way of saying, "They tried to defeat it, and they failed."

Cross-examination debate can be challenging. But knowing how to ask tough questions, how to answer questions effectively, and how to use the cross-examination in your speech will improve your performance at this style of debate.

Chapter 10: Keys to Success

✔ **Ask direct, leading questions to get the answers you want**. This method allows you to control the cross-examination. Open-ended questions give your competitor an opportunity to ramble, taking up your valuable cross-examination time.

✔ **Have a clear objective for your cross-examination**. Ask a series of questions designed to get at a particular point or admission. Start with questions that setup the line of questioning, and then proceed to questions that get to the heart of the matter.

✔ **Answer directly, but be sure to qualify your answers**. A simple "yes" or "no" gives the cross-examiner excessive control over the questioning period. Providing a brief explanation will clarify your perspective and will make it more difficult for your opponent to go on the attack.

✔ **Use the cross-examination**. If you've forced a damaging admission or defended your case effectively, remind your judges about it during the speech that follows.

CHAPTER 11

Foray into Forums:
Standing Out from the Crowd

Coming Up!

Debates don't only take place between two teams. There are often many different perspectives at play. This chapter will show you how to emerge as a leader in forums. You'll find out how to set the agenda, strike a compromise, build a coalition, and speak in an engaging way.

WHEN TWO SIDES AREN'T ENOUGH

Having only an Affirmative team and a Negative team has certain advantages. The issue is clear, especially after the first speaker defines the terms. There's an obvious fault line that divides the opposing teams. Since each side knows exactly what it has to argue, this format certainly makes for good practice and competition.

But do most debates have only two perspectives? If you think about the world around you, you'll realize that there are usually many views on the same subject. Even on the same subject, there are many different sub-issues, and each stakeholder will consider different sub-issues to be the most important ones. Below are descriptions of some of the instances when there are multiple perspectives at play.

Student Congress and Model Parliament

In democratic systems, there are numerous political parties. Each party has elected members who represent its positions in a legislature. In some instances, such as the United States Congress, there are two dominant parties. In other places, such as Canada and many European nations, there are three or more groups represented in significant numbers. A party doesn't only represent a single, narrowly defined perspective on each issue. Rather, its members represent a range of views on what's called the political spectrum. They come together as a unit because their views are reasonably similar, but there's still plenty of room for maneuvering.

In a Student Congress or Model Parliament, the core activities include developing, debating, and voting on Bills. Multiple perspectives go into the drafting of a Bill. Everyone will want to have their issues and views included. If the party proposing the Bill doesn't have a majority in the legislature, it will have to compromise or form a coalition with other members. Consequently, the backroom deal-making is often as important as the debate itself.

Model United Nations

In this international forum, you represent a country on a committee, such as the Security Council or the Commission on Human Rights. Generally, there are only one or two members advocating for your country on each committee. Therefore, deciding on your country's perspective is much easier than deciding on a party's perspective in a Student Congress or Model Parliament. The challenge lies in finding areas of mutual interest and agreement between countries. It's virtually impossible for one country to push through a rigid view, since other countries are unlikely to agree. This makes negotiation and compromise central to the debate.

Committee Meetings

Whether it's a school club, a student council, or a community group, you're probably part of a committee. When a committee meets, its members have goals that are more widely held among participants than in the types of forums mentioned previously. There tends not to be distinct factions. Rather, the debates are more civil and constructive, and the purpose is to decide how best to carry out the group's mandate. You shouldn't be trying to defeat anyone else on the committee, as the aim is to find consensus among all group members. Success in this type of forum debate involves leadership and engagement. Shouting down arguments made by other members is bound to isolate you and render you less effective.

Class Discussions

You've certainly been part of classroom debates on the theme of a novel or on an international affairs issue. Perhaps you've even advocated how to go about solving a math problem or conducting a science experiment. In these discussions, your goals should be to contribute to the learning of everyone in the class, to increase your own understanding of an issue, and to practice your speech and debate skills. Since you're debating with people who are your friends, the style of debate is more constructive and analytical than confrontational. There are no 'winners' and 'losers', but select people will be seen as leaders by their teacher and by their peers. Your mission should be to make sure that you're one of these people.

> **Success Tip!**
>
> Contribute actively to class discussions.

A TRICKY BALANCING ACT

In a debate between two teams, the goals are simple: build your arguments and defeat your opponent's arguments. One team will win, and the other will lose. The only person you have to work with is your partner. Simply put, it's an 'us vs. them' battle.

A forum debate is much different. Not only are you trying to present your arguments, you're also aiming to work within the context of a dynamic debate to see where your points fit in and make the most impact. There are more than two distinct perspectives, making the areas of contention less clear.

You have to work with other people—*engage* rather than *defeat*—in order to achieve your objectives. In fact, your peers will have significant sway in how you're judged, as opposed to a panel of judges who are removed from the debate itself.

All of these factors require you to perform a balancing act. You have to push your perspective, but compromise may be necessary for anything to pass. Being decisive will help you stand out, but other people will want to feel that you're listening to their views. You should strive to set the agenda by promoting the issues you feel are most important, while at the same time ensuring that your comments fit with the debate. In short, people actually have to like you and want to stand with you on the topics being debated.

> **Success Tip!**
>
> Build relations before the forum even starts.

HOME-FIELD ADVANTAGE: SET THE AGENDA

The more involved you are in deciding what gets debated, the more influential you will be in the debate itself. There's rarely enough time to discuss every relevant issue in detail. If there are several important matters, an agenda helps structure and focus the debate. In some cases, there is a formal agenda, such as a list of Bills in a Model Parliament or a list of discussion items in a committee meeting. At other times, the agenda is more informal. The participants who lead the

> **Success Tip!**
>
> Strive to influence what gets debated.

debate essentially set the tone for everyone by making it clear what the key issues are. Here are some strategies that will help you participate in setting the agenda:

Jump on an issue quickly. If you're one of the first people to suggest a reasonable agenda for the debate, your issues are far more likely to be accepted. Once the key issues have been decided, adding your items to the debate may be seen as complicating and sidetracking the forum. The most effective debaters try to set the agenda before the forum even begins. They talk informally with others beforehand to gauge the mood and to suggest ideas. In a crisis committee involving rapidly unfolding events, such as a United Nations Security Council session, tackling a new event quickly will help you set the tone of the discussion to follow.

Explain why your issues are the important ones. In a sense, you're arguing why your issues need to be argued. You need to make it clear to everyone else what the forum stands to gain from debating the issues that you're suggesting. Below are some of the reasons why an issue might need to be debated promptly:

• *Urgency*: If a problem is immediate or forthcoming, claiming urgency can be a compelling reason to have your issue on the agenda. For example, an imminent civil war or a tight project deadline could be cause for urgent debate.

• *Scale*: By explaining the magnitude of a situation, you can present a powerful case to the forum for debating this issue. The enormities of a drug trafficking problem or a growing health crisis are instances in which the scale of the situation can be used to justify discussion.

• *Dependency*: In many cases, a number of important issues are dependent on the outcome of another debate. Say that a Student Council is discussing a year-end party. Debating how much should be spent on it should come before planning other items.

Think about what others will find important. How successful you are in establishing the key issues for debate depends on the opinions of other participants. Judging what other people believe is a valuable tool for proposing an agenda. One method is considering their roles and how they relate to important issues. If you're in a Model Parliament and the Green Party is heavily represented, it's a fair bet that environmental issues will be of foremost concern. But there's a less speculative method of gauging the mood: ask them. It may seem like common sense, but it's rarely done. When you're talking to people before the forum, ask them what they see as the key issues. Listening is far more effective than mind-reading.

COMMON GROUND: STRIKING A COMPROMISE

You think you're right, and you're convinced that everyone else around you should take your view. Unfortunately, they all have their own views and—you guessed it—they think they're right as well. What to do?

Of course, you could go on with the same course, stubbornly sticking to your original position. But consider that you probably need the support of people who have other views. Good luck trying to get your fellow participants to back down and bow to your demands. Usually, you'll have to find common ground and arrive at a compromise. Here are some strategies for coming up with a mutually agreeable position:

> **Success Tip!**
>
> Understand what motivates other participants.

Come into the negotiation from a position of strength. At first, stake out a clear, decisive position. It's impossible to get even part of what you want if you begin with a watered-down version of what you really think. If you start with a position that's already a compromise, you'll probably have to concede even more ground to those who are pushing for a different perspective.

Think about when you used to negotiate with your parents for money to go out. (Or perhaps you still do.) You asked for $40, they proposed $20, and so you comprised at $30. What if you decided to start low, thinking you would be rewarded for being reasonable? You asked for $30, they proposed $20, and so they felt that a $25 compromise would be fair. Next time, you'll remember to start the negotiation a bit higher.

> **Watch Out!**
>
> Don't compromise or give in too quickly.

Stick firm to your most important demands. Know what you consider a top priority and what's less important. Even if you appear to take strong positions on the lower priority demands, you can use them as bargaining chips to protect what you consider vital. A demand that's less important to you may be a concession that someone with another perspective values greatly.

STRENGTH IN NUMBERS: BUILDING COALITIONS

Working alone, it's rather difficult to reach your objectives in a forum. You may prefer to 'go it alone' and get all of the bragging rights if your proposal is accepted. Unfortunately, trying to be the only shining star will rarely work. Even if other people agree with you, they're less likely to vote for your ideas if they think you're trying to dominate.

> **Watch Out!**
>
> Don't appear to be forming exclusive cliques.

A coalition can be an effective vehicle for advancing your interests. Unlike compromising, which emphasizes bringing *ideas* together, coalition-building places more stress on bringing *people* together to promote a set of ideas. Coalitions are usually created *before* the debate, whereas compromises happen *during* the debate. In this sense, a political party is a type of coalition. Building a coalition is tricky, but the effort usually pays off by making it easier to achieve your objectives. Here are some strategies to help you build coalitions:

> **Watch Out!**
>
> Don't form coalitions purely on friendship.

Identify people with similar interests. Although it's rare for any two participants to have exactly the same position on a topic, it's common for numerous people to have positions with minor differences that can be bridged. For example, take a Model United Nations debate on foreign aid. One potential coalition is a group of wealthy donor nations, each having different proposals, but sharing the perspective that aid should be tied to democratic reform.

Make trade-offs to secure passage. Some coalition scenarios involve sacrifices and deals. Separate groups agree to back each other so that each one can accomplish its priorities. For example, the Conservative

Party in a Model Parliament could agree to the Liberal Party's bid for greater spending on health care. In exchange, it would receive a guarantee of the Liberal Party's support for its tax cut proposals.

Share responsibility and credit with other participants. Playing a leadership role doesn't mean hogging the initiative. Trying to dominate a coalition is a sure way to see it fall apart. Everyone is in the coalition because they feel there's something for them to gain. If they see it as a power grab on your part, they may not want to work with you. The best leaders in a coalition work to involve everyone. When an initiative succeeds, the entire team takes credit.

> **Success Tip!**
>
> Identify your potential allies from the outset.

ENGAGE EVERYONE: STYLE AND DELIVERY

Most of the principles of strong delivery discussed in previous chapters hold true in forums, but there are a number of techniques that are particularly important in a group situation. Here are some tips to help you appeal to a wide range of people:

Face as many people as possible. Focusing predominantly on the Chairperson, the front of the room, or the key players is a natural instinct. This practice leaves everyone else feeling 'left out' of your speech. Turning your body and your eyes toward as wide a spectrum of your audience as possible is a great way to keep all of the participants feeling engaged.

At a meeting, sitting at certain positions will help you face the maximum number of people. Sitting at certain positions? You're probably thinking, "It's a table, and you sit down anywhere. It's that simple." Actually, if you look carefully around a typical meeting table, you'll find that certain places are advantageous. These 'power positions' make it more likely that others will notice you when you want to speak. And when you do speak, fewer people will have to turn their bodies in order to face you directly.

Keep you palms open and up. The excessive use of closed-fisted or finger-pointing gestures paints an image of you saying, "Here's why you're wrong." You're essentially placing a 'barrier' between you and everyone else. Speaking with open palms that face up or outward is a way of communicating, "I'm inviting you to join my position." Sounds subtle and subconscious? Well, it is. But it's a small tool that can add an extra touch to your delivery.

Show that you're listening. In a forum, you're communicating even when you're not speaking. Since there are so many speakers with different opinions, everyone is struggling to stand out and to feel that they're having an impact. Eye contact with the speaker and an attentive posture are two ways to show that you're paying atten-

Success Tip!

Stay humble to gain respect and support.

tion. Additionally, everyone likes to know that their contributions are being appreciated by the other participants. Nodding in agreement helps convey engagement and interest in the speaker's comments. In a parliamentary forum, applauding by banging on your desk or chanting, "Here, here!" are other ways to show your agreement.

If you remember the tips and tricks outlined in this chapter, you'll give yourself a competitive advantage as you participate in any type of competitive or informal debate forum.

Chapter 11: Keys to Success

✔ **Provide a sense of direction to the discussion**. Suggest what needs to be discussed or what challenges should be addressed. If the forum focuses on your issues, it's more likely that you'll play a leadership role in the debate.

✔ **Keep your comments in the context of the forum**. Unless you can show why a new direction is necessary, stay focused on the issue at hand. Don't bring up points just because you've wanted to say them for some time.

✔ **Seek common ground with other participants**. Although stating your ideas confidently is important, it's essential that you're able to bring together a coalition of people or to create agreement around key ideas. Play a leadership role by suggesting ways to join forces.

✔ **Listen to what others are saying and respond accordingly**. Since the people you're trying to convince are part of the debate, you need to understand all of the relevant perspectives. Strive to understand what's motivating other participants and adapt your tactics and contributions accordingly.

CHAPTER 12
Wars of Words:
Debates with Commentary

Coming Up!

In this section, you'll see the tips and tricks discussed in previous chapters come together as full debates. The resolutions will be debated vigorously from both sides of the issue so that you can see how a debate unfolds. The commentary and flow sheets will help you understand the tools that the debaters are using. However, you're encouraged to make your own flow sheet as you read each debate.

PARLIAMENTARY STYLE DEBATE: THIS HOUSE WOULD (THW) LOWER THE MINIMUM VOTING AGE.

Debate

Commentary

Speaker: I call this House to order. The Bill before us today is: This House would (THW) lower the minimum voting age. Representing the Government are the Prime Minister and the Minister of the Crown, and representing Her Majesty's Loyal Opposition are the Member of the Opposition and the Leader of the Opposition. I now call upon the Prime Minister to define the terms of the Bill and present the Government's case.

No need for a plan because the resolution is a single, simple decision.

Prime Minister: Thank you, Mr. Speaker. Honorable members of the House, we are here today to debate whether this House should lower the minimum voting age. In order to focus the debate on nations with long-standing democratic traditions, we are referring to the 30 nations that are members of the Organization for Economic Cooperation and Development (OECD), largely North America and Western Europe. We define "lower the minimum voting age" as allowing citizens to vote in elections for public office beginning at the age of 16, compared to the current systems which typically have a minimum voting age of 18 years.

Should state in proper resolution format.

Appropriate rationale and choice for geographic scope.

Good to be specific in this way.

I will focus on the issue of rights—why it is that citizens as young as age 16 *deserve* to vote. My partner will focus on the benefits to society and to young people of lowering the voting age to 16.

Tells the judges exactly where the case is going.

The first point of the Government's case is that people as young as age 16 have adult and democratic responsibilities which should

Clear statement of the point being made.

translate into the right to vote. The concept of rights and responsibilities are related. As someone's responsibilities to society increase, so should the constitutional rights they have to shape how society is run. For example, people as young as 16 pay sales taxes on their rapidly growing spending and income taxes on part-time employment income. They are held criminally responsible, commonly as adults, for actions that violate the law. Society expects these individuals to begin acting like adults, which is why people as young as 16 deserve the right to influence political decisions concerning, for instance, how their tax dollars are spent and a variety of other important issues.

Good connection between rights and responsibilities.

Example helps to clarify the point.

Started with a concluding line, but then moved needlessly back into specifics.

Leader of the Opposition: "On that point" (Prime Minister accepts the Point of Information). "Would you not agree that a basic, easy to perform obligation such as paying taxes or behaving lawfully is fundamentally different than an important, complex choice like deciding on who should govern the country?"

Good timing, as argument has just finished.

Strong contrast between circumstances.

Prime Minister: Firstly, paying taxes and lawful behavior are critically important to the functioning of society. Secondly, as I will discuss later, the premise of your question—voting is too difficult for young people to understand—is completely incorrect.

Now that we have established the issue of democratic rights, we will move on to our second point, which is how significantly political decisions impact young people. The concept of a democratic society is that the people who are impacted by political decisions should be able to determine who it is that makes these decisions. In this sense, we have government by consent of the people. For example, politi-

Speaker foreshadows what's to come, allowing him to move on.

Clear, effective transition back to the speech and to the next point.

Appeal to a widely held belief.

cians make decisions that impact the school system, policing of violence by young people, and access and affordability of college and university. Many youth are also impacted by issues such as poverty, health care, and social services. In order for politicians to have full legitimacy in making these decisions, the youth who are impacted by these choices should be part of the voting constituency that forms our governments.

Since we have now talked about the concept of responsibilities and the numerous political decisions that impact youth, we will now move on to the third and final area of rights, namely whether people as young as 16 have the capability to exercise this right well. The often stated reason for having age 18 as the minimum voting age is that it is at this stage in life that people have the capability to exercise their democratic rights appropriately. It is, of course, reasonable to limit rights to people so young that they cannot exercise them responsibly. However, this is not the case for students who are 16 years old. People at this age are learning about society and government at school, arguably giving them more recent knowledge about political issues than even many adults. In addition, they have had many years to learn about how society and the political system work. They are beginning to think about what they want to do after graduating from school, such as earning a living or pursuing college or university education. That is, they have the capability to think rationally and responsibly about how to exercise this important right.

Member of the Opposition: "Point of Information" (Prime Minister accepts). "Do you not think that people should finish learning all

Examples provide context as to why the rights are important.

Links the initial concept of impact to the concept of legitimacy.

Signal that the speaker wants to debunk a common myth.

Why not go right into how voting at age 16 is okay?

Have most youth been paying attention for these "many years?"

Is there really a definite time when you have 'learned' the concepts of voting?

of these important matters before they vote, as opposed to getting familiar with political decision *while* they are allowed to vote?"

Prime Minister: The right to vote has never required a sophisticated level of political knowledge. Rather, one must have merely enough information to make their preferred choice, and the Government believes that a 16 year old student's school environment provides sufficient knowledge for a carefully considered voting decision.

Good description of what the broader concept of voting rights means (and doesn't mean).

I have told you firstly that the right to vote is a logical extension of the responsibilities placed on people as young as 16, secondly that political decisions have a strong impact on students of this age, and finally that they have the capability to exercise this right appropriately. Therefore, the Government has established the theme of rights, which is why this House should lower the minimum voting age to 16. Thank you, Mr. Speaker.

Numbering the points helps the judges to remember them.

Clear tie-back to the main theme and case statement.

Speaker: I thank the Prime Minister for his remarks. I now call upon on the Member of the Opposition to deliver her speech.

Member of the Opposition: Thank you, Mr. Speaker. Today, the Government has presented a case based on the assumption that there is a democratic right to vote at the age of 16. After refuting the three arguments presented by the Prime Minister, I will talk about the idea of the ability to vote responsibly. My partner will talk about the concept of what influences a vote, and how this makes lowering the voting age a bad idea.

Immediately stakes out an approach to the refutation.

"Bad" is too elementary a term.

The first argument made by the Prime Minister was that young people have adult responsibilities, which means they should

Tells the judges what's being refuted.

have the adult right to vote. In reality, however, society sets different age limits for different activities and responsibilities, depending on the circumstances. The reason why people pay sales taxes and income taxes at a younger age is that they have the ability to spend and earn income before they are 18 years old. On the other hand, the right to purchase alcohol or buy cigarettes is restricted to people who are several years older, because society does not believe that young people have enough knowledge or experience to make these decisions responsibly. Teenagers are often treated as adults by the criminal system because by the age of 16 society believes that they know the difference between right and wrong. However, it's wrong to equate each of these circumstances to the right to vote in how society at large operates. The Prime Minister has tried to draw parallels that have no direct relation to one another, which is why this first argument is invalid.

Effective explanations of the distinctions between the Prime Minister's examples.

Could have been a bit more concise, or cut out one example.

Why is it wrong?

Then, the Prime Minister went on to talk about the political decisions impacting young people. If we extend this logic, then why would we not lower the voting age to people much younger than 16, who were also affected by a wide variety of public policy issues? The reason is that until the age of 18, we entrust parents or guardians to act on behalf of their children. Parents or guardians take the interests of their families into consideration when making political decisions, and are considered to be representatives of the entire family unit. This second argument, therefore, lacks both logical consistency and necessity.

Stretching the logic is a good way to show the point's flaws.

Do they look at what their children want, or just what they want for themselves?

Prime Minister: "On that point" (Member of the Opposition accepts). "Isn't it true that by age 16, a student has reached significant independence from his or her parents, particularly their views of society and the world?"

Independent thought being a central tenet of the right to vote.

Member of the Opposition: Legally, we still consider a 16 year old to be under the care of his or her parents or guardians. Surely, they are developing independence, but they have not yet reached the stage of full independence required in order for them to make a fully independent voting choice

But is legal custody the real issue here?

The Prime Minister's third point was that people as young as 16 have the capability to vote responsibly. However, even he himself acknowledged that young people are in the process of learning the required knowledge and are only *beginning* to think in the long-term about various matters concerning their lives. We can't equate this level of knowledge and experience to that of an adult.

Using the Prime Minister's own words to attack the case.

Clash with this point was short, but to the point nonetheless.

This leads me very well into the theme of the constructive part of my speech, which is whether students as young as age 16 have the ability to exercise the voting right responsibly. As the Government has stated, we can only extend the right to vote to those who can exercise this important practice appropriately, and reasonable limits are certainly in order if they can't do so.

Clear shift from clash to constructive.

My first argument is that minors are not yet familiar with the complex decisions that are involved in independent living. They have not yet had to manage a household, as they are still generally under the care of their parents or guardians. They don't take care of maintaining the family residence, nor how the family spends its income. As a result, they don't have the experience in independent decision-making necessary to have the right to make decisions on the wide variety of issues that impact families.

Need to explain why experience living independently matters to the right to vote.

Rambling sentence.

In addition to having insufficient experience, my second point is that they have insufficient engagement in the political process to vote wisely. Most youth are more interested in music, sports, and socializing than debating the public policy issues that impact society. In fact, even people several years over the age of 18 who are allowed to vote have shown substantial disengagement, considering that voter turnout at this age level is significantly lower than for older adults. It is only once people enter the 'real world' of work and post secondary education that they become more engaged in societal and political issues, rather than primarily entertainment and educational matters.

Minister of the Crown: "Point of Information" (Member of the Opposition accepts). "So are you suggesting that retired seniors who are more concerned with relaxation and vacations should have their right to vote taken away because they are not in what you call the 'real world' of work?"

Member of the Opposition: The Minister of the Crown makes a rather trivial comparison that has little impact on our argument. Senior citizens have already had extensive life experience and know what it means to exercise a democratic right to vote. The same cannot be said for someone who's only 16 years old.

In my speech, I have shown you that the Prime Minister has not sufficiently proven his points about the democratic responsibilities and rights, the impact of political decisions, and the capability to exercise the voting right responsibly. I have presented a case based on the ability to vote, starting with the lack of familiarity with independent decision-mak-

Good transition from life experience to engagement.

Use of related facts as basis for an argument.

Draws a parallel to an idea most would consider ridiculous, thereby implying a flaw in logic.

Good contrast between seniors and students to answer the Point of Information.

Effective because it says specifically what has been refuted.

ing, and continuing with how people as young as 16 years old have insufficient engagement in the political process to make informed voting choices. For these reasons, we proudly oppose this Bill.

May be helpful to number the points.

Speaker: I thank the Member of the Opposition. I now call upon the Minister of the Crown to continue the Government's case.

Minister of the Crown: Mr. Speaker, the Opposition has claimed that students under the age of 18 do not have the ability to make an informed decision, which I intend to refute in my speech. Once I have proven this theme to be incorrect, I will continue the Government's case by discussing three additional reasons for change centering on the idea of benefits to society, particularly young people.

Good 'road map' for the speech.

The first point made by the Member of the Opposition was that young people are not yet familiar with living on their own. This argument certainly doesn't demonstrate that students at least 16 years old would be incapable of making decisions that affect how people live. One does not necessarily have to be directly involved in making every decision to be able to understand decisions and their impact. In fact, senior citizens who are under the care of their children or a nursing home are certainly not forbidden from exercising their independent judgment. Similarly, we do not prevent people who are ill or hospitalized from exercising their democratic will. The Government only has to show that younger voters would be capable of understanding the choices that impact society, and their experience up to the age of 16 and their education on civic matters is, in our view, sufficient to be able to make an informed vote.

Draws clear distinction between making and understanding decisions.

Example illustrates how custody or care doesn't necessarily impede judgment.

Clarifies the Government's responsibility.

The Opposition's second point was that young people are insufficiently engaged to be able to make a wise choice. But perhaps, Mr. Speaker, the reason why many youth are not engaged is that their voices are not considered in the political dynamic. Of course, many adults are not engaged in the political system, but society certainly would not take away their right to vote based on a litmus test of their level of engagement. In reality, there are people at all age groups who are disinterested in the political system, and these individuals are unlikely to vote by their own choice. Therefore, the Opposition's point makes a sweeping generalization that doesn't stand up to logical examination.

Suggests the result is a symptom rather than proof of an argument.

Shows how the Opposition's logic could, if extended, lead to an unthinkable practice.

Clear statement of why the argument is incorrect.

Now that I have clashed with the Opposition's case, I would like to build on the Prime Minister's case by discussing the benefits of allowing younger people to vote. My first point is that allowing people to vote once they are 16 years old will force politicians to represent more actively the issues that affect this age demographic. Politicians are most responsive to the needs of their constituents when these constituents can determine whether or not they remain in office. Parents only consider youth issues as one of many issues, and students may have views that are indeed different than those of their parents. By lowering the voting age, politicians would have to consider, for example, the views of students on how to improve the education system or how to promote sports and fitness among young people. As a result, an underrepresented segment of society would have their issues advanced by elected officials.

Smart to go into why the principle matters.

Links motivations to behaviors.

Specific example of how the change would have an impact.

Member of the Opposition: "On that point, sir" (Minister of the Crown accepts). "So, then, if

16 year old voters want more days off from school, fewer classes each day, and longer breaks between each class, should politicians cater to this so grossly underrepresented segment of our society?"

Uses the Minister of the Crown's own logic against her.

Minister of the Crown: I think that the Member of the Opposition is trivializing and exaggerating how the system works. Politicians have to make reasonable decisions after listening carefully to all stakeholder groups, including students, teachers, parents, and administrators. There is no reason to believe that they would give in to unrealistic demands.

Explains how multiple stakeholders are a 'check' on one having undue influence.

In addition to having their issues better represented, my second point is that students will become more politically involved. Since students at this age are learning about civic engagement in their classes, they will have an opportunity to put what they have learned in practice as voters. If somebody knows that their views count and that their choices can have an impact on their lives, they are far more likely to take an interest in, and to become involved in, the political system that shapes these decisions. We contend that young people will spend more time debating and discussing among themselves and within their families the important issues that affect society, which is why we believe that lowering the voting age will promote positive democratic engagement.

Connects with a point made by the Prime Minister.

Provides insight into human motivations.

Reminds judges of the theme being discussed.

Finally, the third argument under this benefits theme is that allowing people to vote at a young age will create not only short-term, but more importantly, long-term participation in the democratic process. We all know that people tend to form habits, likes, and dislikes relatively early on in life. If young people become engaged before they even finish

Could political parties make promises that entice them into long-term loyalty when they're at an impressionable age?

school, they are far more likely to participate in the electoral system as voters, volunteers, and activists later on in life. Overall, this creates a more politically aware society in which more citizens are continually interested in the issues that affect them and are willing to hold politicians to account.

Discussing impact on society as a whole strengthens the claim of benefits.

I want to come back to the Member of the Opposition's refutation and defend some of the arguments that the Prime Minister made. To the Prime Minister's first point about rights and responsibilities, the Member of the Opposition admitted that students age 16 or over are expected to know right from wrong in terms of criminal behavior, so why would they be any less capable of judging right from wrong in terms of decisions that others, such as politicians, make? Regarding the Prime Minister's second point about political decisions directly impacting young people, the Opposition stated that parents should have exclusive right to judge what is best for people under 18 years old. However, at 16 years old, in individual exercises a significant degree of independence in his or her daily life, as parental influence gets weaker over time. On the Prime Minister's final point about the capability to exercise the democratic rights appropriately, the Opposition argued that people are only learning about several important decisions at age 16. However, society does not require adult voters to be fully informed, and indeed many of them are also learning at the same time. In fact, it is a good thing that students would be learning about political decisions at the same time as having to make the voting choice, which makes the decision more engaged and more informed.

Draws a parallel.

This line of defense has already been discussed in the debate.

In general, these points of defense are quite brief and don't add significant value.

The only really 'new' claim made in this paragraph.

In my speech, I have talked to you about the benefits of politicians representing youth issues, students becoming more politically involved, and creating long-term habits of political engagement. Then, I showed you why the Opposition's points regarding the ability to make decisions are incorrect, and why the Opposition's refutation of the Prime Minister's points concerning the right to vote did not weaken the case. Therefore, we stand proudly for this Bill.

Number the points to make it clearer for the judges.

Speaker: I thank the Minister the Crown for her remarks, and I now call upon the Leader of the Opposition to complete the constructive part of the Opposition's case and to deliver the Opposition's rebuttal.

Leader of the Opposition: Thank you, Mr. Speaker. I want to begin my address by presenting the final two points of the Opposition's case, after which I will refute the Government's new points and tell you why we have won this debate. Our new constructive arguments focus on the theme of what influences a young person's vote, and why these influences would have a negative impact should people be allowed to vote at the age of 16.

Shows how the Leader of the Opposition is going to add value to the case.

Firstly, media and political pressures, that is, external influences, have a greater impact on a minor than on an adult. The younger we are, the less experienced we are in seeing through some of the rhetoric that is presented to us by commentators and politicians. Students are less likely to have significant experience analyzing media stories and deciding what they believe to be true and what is false or exaggerated. Therefore, a vote by someone under age 18 would be less independent given these external influences.

Good discussion of human psychology.

Backs up theoretical claims with the experience factor.

Secondly, Mr. Speaker, there are also personal influences that can significantly impact the students vote. When they are under the age of 18, individuals are guided to a large extent by teachers and parents. A student can easily be swayed by the class discussion or by a teacher's natural, unintentional biases in formal and informal instruction on politics and government. Additionally, a parent has significant influence on how their children think about many issues, shaped in part by their discussions at the dinner table, for example. For these reasons, the full independence of the voting decision would be compromised by these significant personal influences.

But aren't schools meant to teach students how to think critically?

Links back to the central concept of a vote needing to be independent.

Prime Minister: "Point of Information!" (Leader of the Opposition accepts). "Since when do 16 year old students simply parrot whatever their parents do and think? In fact, aren't they at an age when they actively try to be more independent from their parents?"

Cites a commonly held belief, probably understood by many in the room.

Leader of the Opposition: While they are certainly in the process of becoming more independent, their parents have had and continue to have significant influence over a child's views, in large part because of how much time a family spends together.

Uses a careful concession to explain difference between partial and full independence.

I now want to go into the new points brought up by the Minister of the Crown. His first point was that politicians will be more likely to represent youth issues, but that could simply lead to politicians making unrealistic promises to this voting group. Since minors are much less involved in the broader issues that affect society at large then adults, they would be making their decisions on a more narrow set of interests.

Explains why this is a narrow voting block.

The second point was that students will become more politically involved. It seems like the Government wants to have it both ways, saying on the one hand that they are informed enough to make good decisions, and saying on the other hand that they need to become more involved in order to make good decisions. Addressing this point directly, however, a youth who is interested in political issues certainly has an incentive to become informed knowing that they will be able to vote in only a few years. In fact, many young people get involved in areas other than voting, such as volunteering on election campaigns, writing letters to the editor, or talking to their family and friends about their views on different issues.

Points out an apparent inconsistency in the Government's case.

Would more people want to participate in these activities if they could vote?

So, Mr. Speaker, what have we heard in today's debate, and what has this debate come down to? The first competing theme of this debate was the idea of rights versus the ability to exercise these rights responsibly. The Government based its case on the logic that just because people under the age of 18 have other rights and responsibilities, they should necessarily have the voting right, whereas we have talked about why the right to vote in elections requires a level of knowledge and experience that is different from other areas. Elections are about much more than individual behavior, as they shape our entire economy, society, and culture. The Government has staked their claim on the idea that simply being in the process of learning something is sufficient to make an informed choice, while we've argued that knowledge and experience are prerequisites to having the right to make this important choice. The Government would have you believe that voting is just another part of a teenager's learning experience. We believe that voting is so important to our society that we cannot simply allow it to be just another learning process.

Signals a transition into the rebuttal portion of the speech.

Draws a contrast between how the theme was discussed by the respective sides.

Continues to draw good distinctions between approaches, tilting them in a pro-Opposition way.

The Government's case regarding benefits to society is based on the notion that creating another narrow interest group makes our democratic system work better. The fundamental reason why parents still guide their kids until the age of 18 is that society does not want people to be getting their way on every issue before this age, but politicians would have to give in to the will of people as young as age 16 if they are given the right to vote. This may not serve the interests of families and society as a whole, which is what adults are better able to judge who should be in power. We talked about how influences from the media, politicians, parents, and teachers could distort voting choices that are supposed to be independent. An independent choice is the basis of a truly democratic society, a choice that must be fully informed and based on sound judgment.

Shift to the next theme, but it could be made clearer that this is the case.

But, then, wouldn't politicians consider the views of everyone else who supposedly doesn't want minors to get their way on everything?

Ties the refutation back to this key principle of the case.

Mr. Speaker, what does the Prime Minister have to do in his rebuttal? Firstly, he has to show you how somebody at the age of 16 who is still in school and still under the guidance of his or her parents somehow has the independent life experience necessary to judge wider societal issues. Secondly, he has to show you how people at such a young age are possibly able to know as much about the complex and wide variety of political issues, such as international trade and taxation policy, as adults who have many more years of knowledge and experience regarding these matters. Thirdly, he must be able to show you how exactly a teenager's vote could be as independent as an adult's vote, considering the range of influences that shape a person's mind and behavior at this stage in their lives. We are confident that we have shown you why the Government has not sufficiently proven its case on these three

Frames the debate and possibly throws off the Prime Minister.

Opposition using this criterion because it feels it has prevailed on the issue.

Criterion implies why the Prime Minister can't win on this dimension.

In general, an attempt to place the burden squarely on the Government.

core issues, which is why we oppose this Bill. Thank you, Mr. Speaker.

Speaker: I thank the Leader of Her Majesty's Loyal Opposition first constructed speech and rebuttal, and now call upon the Prime Minister to conclude today's debate.

Prime Minister: Thank you, Mr. Speaker. Let me get right to the heart of what this debate is *really* about. Can a right as fundamental and beneficial as the right to vote be arbitrarily taken away on the basis that someone is not completely self-sufficient and has not learned about the complexities of every political issue? The right to vote is not based on the idea that someone has to be perfectly informed about every issue, and restricting this right is only justified if granting it would be harmful or completely unjustified.

What the Opposition has told us today is that perhaps young people need a little bit more living experience, a little bit more engagement, and a little bit less influence by other people. One could argue that these very same desires hold true for so many people in the current voting population. Of course, we would not take away the central right to vote because an adult has not fully met all of the desirable criteria of a completely informed voter. The heart of a democratic system is that the voter is always right and that nobody else can pass judgment on a voter's ability to make sound judgments.

We have shown you that because young people have many of the same responsibilities as adults and are affected by the decisions that politicians make, granting them the right to vote would be entirely appropriate. We have shown you that 16 year olds

Prime Minister is trying to seize back the agenda, not going to play into the Opposition's trap.

Good choice to describe it as a single, central issue, even if it combines several themes.

Describes how the Opposition made weak distinctions.

More effective to rework the previous sentence than to be defensive like this.

Saying "the heart" suggest that this is a central factor.

Good use of parallel language with "We have shown you."

have sufficient knowledge through their education to be able to exercise this right appropriately. And we have shown you today that the benefits of giving younger citizens this fundamental democratic right will encourage elected politicians to represent their issues well, and that it will encourage young people to become more engaged in the political system now and in the long-term. Therefore, we stand proudly for this Bill.

Sentence is slightly too drawn out.

Speaker: I thank all of the debaters for their remarks. This House is now adjourned.

COMMENTARY ON "VOTING AGE" DEBATE

Both teams presented well-organized cases that were easy to follow. Examples were used heavily to support claims. However, in some places, broad generalizations were made without sufficient explanation or proof. The Points of Information added character to the debate, as did the direct, point by point clash from both sides.

What did the Government do well?

• *Analysis of roles and responsibilities.* The Prime Minister, in particular, was effective in examining the nature of citizen's place in society at the age of 16, citing examples such as criminal and financial responsibilities. The discussion of capability to exercise this democratic right added weight to the underlying claim.

• *Discussion of results and outcomes.* After the Prime Minister had explained why lowering the voting age was the 'right' decision, the Minister of the Crown explained why it matters. This discussion of impact added depth by showing that the Government case was about more than only theoretical, principles-based arguments. It showed that there was a practical dimension as well.

• *Structure. Structure. Structure.* Both speakers made it absolutely clear where they were going and what they had accomplished, including introductions, conclusions, and transitions. This level of organization took the judges on a well-defined 'path' and made it easy to grasp all of the important concepts.

• *Seizing back the agenda in the rebuttal.* The Leader of the Opposition did an effective job at trying to frame the debate, but the Prime Minister didn't get side-tracked. In the Government's rebuttal, there was a clear, to the point articulation of the key themes and why the Government had come out ahead of these fronts.

What could the Government have improved?

• *Why age 16?* Why not 17, or 15 for that matter? Granted, this is a difficult distinction to make, and the Government did its best with it. But further explanation or evidence as to why this was the 'magic' number would have helped.

• *Defense of previous arguments.* The Minister of the Crown's attempted defense of the Prime Minister's points seemed scattered at times. In many cases, the defense did not add any significant value or depth to the previous arguments. It would have been advantageous to focus on one area where significant damage was done and to present a more thorough defense.

What did the Opposition do well?

• *Discussion of exceptions and nuances.* The Government tried to use examples outside of the core issue of the debate as support for lowering the voting age, which the Opposition dealt with head-on. Both speakers explained how these instances were often generalizations and did not show specifically why allowing 16 year olds to vote would be the right decision to make.

• *Examination of central tenets of democracy.* The Opposition looked at how the independence and solid foundation for a vote was imperative in order for the democratic system to have full legitimacy. Distinctions were drawn to show how not all of the key criteria for a sound vote are fulfilled for a 16 year old.

• *Framing the debate in the rebuttal.* The Leader of the Opposition was very clear and decisive in arguing what the key issues were. Particularly at the end, telling the Prime Minister what the Government's rebuttal must do was a bold, but carefully executed method.

What could the Opposition have improved?

• *Relevance of certain details.* For example, talking about legal custody and its implications for voting decisions, or citing how people under the age of 18 can get involved in other ways were not central to the fundamental question of the right to vote. It's essential that every point ties directly into the case theme.

• *Generalizations and assumptions.* In particular, the Leader of the Opposition's point about parents and teachers influencing students could have included more concrete and specific analysis. Also, when the Member of the Opposition talked about the negative impact of a lack of independent living, there wasn't sufficient analysis to show why specifically this assumption was correct in the context of the debate on lowering the voting age.

VOTING AGE DEBATE: FLOW SHEET

GOVERNMENT	OPPOSITION
Prime Minister (#1)	**Member of the Opposition (#2)**
Definition: Age 16, OECD nations	
1. Age 16 have adult responsibilities	Clash 1: Depends on circumstances
2. Impact of political decisions	Clash 2: Illogical and unnecessary
3. Capability to exercise right	Clash 3: Do not have full knowledge
Minister of the Crown (#3)	
Clash 1: Does not show incapability	1. Inexperience in complex decisions
Clash 2: Sweeping generalization	2. Insufficient political engagement
	Leader of the Opposition (#4)
4. Politicians forced to represent	Clash 4: Narrow set of interests
5. More politically involved	Clash 5: Contradicts Point 3
6. Long-term participation	Clash 6: Speculative at best
Defense 1: Know right from wrong	
Defense 2: Significant independence	
Defense 3: Okay to be learning	4. Media and political pressures
	5. Personal influences on youth
Prime Minister (#5)	
Central issue: Can the right to vote be taken away arbitrarily on the dimensions discussed in the debate?	Criteria 1: Sufficient experience?
	Criteria 2: Knowledge of issues?
	Criteria 3: Independent choice?
Opposition: Youth need a bit more experience, a bit more engagement, and a bit less influence by others	Theme 1: Rights vs. ability to exercise the rights responsibly
Government: Many of the same responsibilities, affected by decisions, sufficient knowledge, and benefits to democratic system	Theme 2: Impact on how the democratic system operates

CROSS-EXAMINATION STYLE DEBATE: BE IT RESOLVED THAT (BIRT) THE CORPORATE SPONSORSHIP OF OUR SCHOOLS IS HARMFUL.

Debate

Chairperson: I call this debate to order. The topic of debate today is: Be it resolved that (BIRT) the corporate sponsorship of our schools is harmful. I would like to welcome the first Affirmative speaker and the second Affirmative speaker, who will support the resolution, and the first Negative speaker and the second Negative speaker, who will oppose the resolution. I now call upon the first speaker of the Affirmative team to define the terms of the resolution and to introduce the Affirmative's case.

First Affirmative: Thank you, Madame Chairperson. The resolution before us today is: Be it resolved that the corporate sponsorship of our schools is harmful. We would like to begin by defining the terms of this resolution. We define "corporate sponsorship" as advertising, direct marketing, exclusive agreements, incentive programs, and event and facility naming rights. We defined "our schools" as all of the public schools in the Freedonia school district. Finally, we define "harmful" as negatively impacting the operation of schools and the education of students. I will tell you why school administration is hurt by corporate sponsorship, and the second Affirmative speaker will tell you why students are harmed by this practice.

    Our first contention is that corporate sponsorship focuses school administrators

Commentary

Clearly a values, 'right or wrong' type of resolution.

Broad but clear definition of corporate sponsorship.

Reasonable limitation, does not change the principles involved.

A sound split between school impact and student impact.

on interests other than what should be the only focus: the best interests of students. With corporate sponsorship, school managers must consider what will yield the maximum revenues, even if that means students may be unfavorably affected by the outcome. So, if a soft drink company is willing to pay for the exclusive right to put vending machines in the school, the school principal may be inclined to accept the offer of funding, even if it harms student health. Schools are including activities and exercises about a product, sponsored by the producer. The "calculate the number of chocolate chips in a bag of 15 cookies" math activity is really marketing for a company. This practice compromises the objectivity of the school curriculum, and encourages educators to consider factors other than what makes for the best learning material. Therefore, the conflict of interest between student learning and corporate interests is unwelcome and harmful.

Good statement of guiding principal for schools.

How do we know they "must" consider maximum revenues?

Need a transition phrase, such as "Another area of concern is that …"

In addition to placing school administrators in a conflict of interest position, corporate sponsorship also impacts the relationship between the government and our school district. That is, the rise in corporate sponsorship of schools sends a signal to the government that schools have another source that they can turn to in the event that public funding is inadequate. As a result, it essentially lets governments 'off the hook' when it comes to providing sufficient funding for our schools. Last year, the Department of Education declined our district's request to increase funding, stating that schools had to explore other sources of revenue. We contend that public funding, which does not come with strings attached, is superior to corporate funding, which allows them influence inside the school.

In the first sentence, say, in general, how it has an impact.

Explain how it sends such a signal to the government.

Could it just be that they didn't have enough money, and were simply suggesting a solution?

Was this the key idea?

Today, I have told you firstly that corporate sponsorship encourages administrators to consider corporate interest even at the expense of student interest, and I have told you secondly that it has a negative impact on government support for public education. Therefore, we stand proudly in favor of the resolution that corporate sponsorship harms our public education system. I now stand open for cross-examination.

Clear statement of what's been discussed.

Second Negative: Do you agree that a principal is responsible first and foremost for ensuring that students learn well?

Shifting the focus away from budget responsibilities.

First Affirmative: Yes, of course, nothing else should provide a conflicting interest.

Implies corporate interests are conflicting.

Second Negative: Would you also agree that parents and school board official judge a principal's effectiveness by how strong of a learning environment he or she creates?

Reinforces the thrust of the first question.

First Affirmative: Yes, but a principal also faces pressure to balance a budget and will certainly pursue whatever means are available to increase revenues.

Strong qualification, evokes what was said in speech.

Second Negative: Is it not true that a principal has a choice to accept or reject corporate sponsorships on a case by case basis?

Leading into key cross-examination goal.

First Affirmative: Yes, although there is always financial pressure on a school to accept corporate sponsorships.

Senses the attack, clearly defends the presence of a conflict.

Second Negative: So, if they are responsible primarily for learning, are evaluated on this basis, and have full authority to make sponsorship agreements, would principals ever

Ties the full line of questioning together to get at the main point.

make an agreement that has an overall negative impact on the school?

First Affirmative: Well, it's clear that they now have to consider multiple interests, and sometimes financial pressures will undoubtedly lead to a negative impact on the school.

Standing firm.

Is it "sometimes" or "undoubtedly?"

Second Negative: Thank you, our time is up.

Chairperson: Thank you. I now call upon the first speaker of the Negative team to introduce its case and, if desired, to contest any of the Affirmative's definitions.

First Negative: Thank you, Madame Chairperson. Ladies and gentlemen, before I introduce our team's case, I would like to take a few minutes to clash with the two points made by the first speaker of the Affirmative team.

A bit too general for the introduction, but does get right into the refutation.

The Affirmative started by talking about how administrators will be placed in a conflict of interest position. However, as brought up in the cross-examination, administrators do not have a mandate to advance corporate interests, nor are they judged in this regard. They are judged by how well students in their school perform and how well they manage the operations of the school. Likewise, curriculum developers are judged by how well educational materials help students learn important concepts, not by how well they promote corporations. Administrators, of course, take into consideration the impact of a variety of corporate sponsorships may have on student learning. If they come to the sound judgment that the benefits of corporate sponsorship, such as funding for important extracurricular activities, are significant and that the corporate advertising would not actually

Reinforces the questions asked in the cross-examination.

Clearly opposes the Affirmative's interpretations of administrator responsibilities.

Sets up the criteria for decision-making based on the principle mentioned above.

harm students, they are perfectly justified in making this choice.

Then, the second Affirmative point was that the government may feel that it has less of an obligation to fund public education. Actually, quite the opposite is true. Schools do not justify corporate sponsorships to parents by saying how it helps pay for basic education materials. Rather, they show how corporate sponsorships help pay for some of the enhancements to education, such as recreational activities and field trips. The government is accountable to the electorate to provide what is necessary for quality student learning, especially for those schools that may not have succeeded in attracting large corporate sponsorships. Indeed, as the government continues to increase funding for education, it ultimately comes out of other valuable programs or results in higher taxes on parents. Instead, corporate sponsorship simply means an additional revenue source without giving up another program or greater part of family income, which makes the Affirmative's argument irrelevant and incorrect.

Now that I have shown you why the way the Affirmative arguments are incorrect, I want to introduce the Negative case by talking about the benefits of corporate sponsorship to schools. My first point, which I have introduced briefly in my clash, is that corporate sponsorship provides valuable funding to schools. Rather than being entirely dependent on what the government provides on a year to year basis, corporate sponsorship allows schools to be proactive in finding the funding to meet their specific needs. For example, if the school wants to host a particular event, it can seek a corporate sponsorship of the event to ensure that it takes place. Or, if

But what if there are budget pressures?

They say it's not the reason, but does that mean it isn't?

Could be argued that these are really a core part of the education.

So if a school falls short, the government just makes up for the difference? Then what's the incentive? And isn't that harmful because it affects other programs and taxes?

Clear statement of the speech's theme.

Should be more specific as to what the point is, "valuable funding" is the whole point of the case.

"Allows?" Or forces?

Good matching of situations and solution.

a school wants to undertake an expansion of its library, it can partner with a company in a shopping incentive program to provide the necessary funding. Therefore, corporate sponsorship can be an important source of funding for enhancements to a school.

Secondly, corporate sponsorship of schools allows educators to have some influence over corporate activities that impact children. If corporations are dependent on schools for some of their marketing efforts, they are far more likely to pay attention to what educators want to see in terms of their practices. For instance, many schools in our district have been demanding that soft drink companies provide healthier alternatives, such as juice and water, in their vending machines. In turn, we have seen healthier alternatives in many of the vending machines in this district's public schools. In one case, a school in our district partnered with an energy company on an environmental initiative, which served the desire of educators to promote environmental awareness and good corporate citizenship. Undoubtedly, corporate sponsorship can provide a win-win situation that allows schools to impact positively the activities of corporations.

In my speech, I have told you why corporate sponsorship does not place school administrators in an unhealthy conflict of interest and that it does not compromise government funding for core programs. I have also told you in our constructive matter that schools benefit from valuable corporate funding and their ability to impact the actions of corporations. For these reasons, we stand proudly in opposition to this resolution, and I am now ready to be cross-examined.

Or perhaps educators now have to pay even more attention to corporations.

Strong example of challenge and result.

First example school-specific, appropriate move into wider benefits to society.

Perhaps say "firstly" and "secondly."

First Affirmative: Is it fair to say that a teacher's main responsibly is, logically, to teach?

Seems a touch too basic, but lays down a key assumption.

First Negative: Yes, obviously.

First Affirmative: And is it also fair to say that a principal's main role is to run the school?

First Negative: Yes, but I really don't see what the point is here.

Let the cross-examiner say what the point is.

First Affirmative: Okay, so you acknowledge that neither teachers nor principals are concerned to a significant extent with trying to change corporations?

Starting to make more sense what the objective is.

First Negative: No, no. In addition to their primary duties, they also want to make sure the overall learning environment is positive.

Establishes that a there is a relevant secondary duty as well.

First Affirmative: But would you not agree that given the choice between funding for what they feel they need to do for their students and some desire to change corporations, they would much rather take care of what they need to do?

First Negative: Well, I think in reality they consider all of the factors.

Explain further.

First Affirmative: So, when considering all of the factors, if principals really wanted to get money for more field trips, they might very well leave their desires to be social activists for other occasions?

Example makes the point more concrete.

First Negative: All I am saying is that within a school environment, at least teachers and administrators have a greater ability to generate a positive impact on corporate activities.

Does ability translate into action?

First Affirmative: Okay, thank you.

Chairperson: I thank the first speaker of the Negative team for her remarks, and I now call upon the second speaker of the Affirmative team to continue the debate.

Second Affirmative: Thank you. Fellow debaters, judges, audience members, and chairperson, my partner started this debate by talking about the negative influence of corporate sponsorship on school administration. Now I want to extend our case by talking about the direct and negative impact of corporate sponsorship on students.

The third argument of the Affirmative case is that kids are far more vulnerable to the effects of advertising. At a young age, people are less able to make informed, critical, and rational decisions about corporate claims. Kids are more likely to believe what a company has to say about its product. Corporate sponsorship of schools allows companies easy access to this vulnerable population, well out of the protective reach of parents. For example, when a textbook contains examples about corporations that were sponsored by corporations, a student sees this information as true. In addition, the fact that the information was provided in an educational setting makes it far less likely that the student is going to question its validity. Also, when students see television advertisements as part of a sponsored daily news program, they often view corporate claims as correct, especially since it's part of their school program. We believe strongly that advertising to an impressionable student population is harmful.

Finally, our fourth argument is that corporate sponsorship distracts attention away

Clear that point can't be taken any further.

Shorten the use of titles.

Helpful link back to what has been accomplished already.

Personalizes the issue of debate more than first speech did.

An easy to understand description of a child's thinking.

The point being, parents and not schools should be the 'gatekeepers'.

Explanation of why information can be harmful.

Would they really accept it any more than an advertisement they see at home?

from learning. It goes without saying that students go to school to learn, not to be hit with corporate messages. In fact, a school is supposed to provide a learning environment for students entirely different than the commercial world around them. If every extracurricular event is sponsored by a company, and if they see corporations trying to sell them products daily within the school, it almost makes schools an extension of the shopping mall as opposed to solely a place to learn. We argue that this makes corporate sponsorship a distraction for students, which makes them focus less on the learning that they are supposed to be focusing on exclusively.

Fits into theme of harming students.

Strong distinction helps to illustrate the argument.

Somewhat of a stretch, but does illustrate the point being made.

Concludes quickly, need to develop more.

So what about the arguments made by the first speaker of the Negative team? Her first point was that corporate sponsorship provides valuable funding for programs, which is obviously the basic element of a sponsorship agreement. But the issue here is really what corporate sponsorship costs the school in terms of its independence and its learning. Every minute that students spend reading poster advertisements or viewing television commercials takes away from time spent on learning. Society places an economic value on this learning time. Also, shopping incentive programs encourage students and parents to buy more, which ends up costing families significantly just to provide a small amount of extra funding to a school program. The question of this debate is whether schools should be giving up part of their core mandate to provide a strong learning environment in exchange for a few nonessential corporate sponsorship dollars each year.

Clear transition into refutation.

Implying the point was more common sense than insight.

Attempt to frame the point of contention.

Suggests that every minute must be put to maximum use.

This isn't the point.

Too early to go into the general "question of this debate."

Are they always nonessential?

Her second argument was that schools can somehow influence corporate activities if there is a sponsorship partnership. This begs the question, who has more power in the relationship? A school which is doing whatever it takes to get more funding, or a large, powerful corporation which is marketing to a wide variety of students by dangling financial benefits to schools? Of course, it's obvious that corporations have far more influence on the habits and behaviors of students in schools could possibly have on how self-interested corporations run. Anyways, social activism is not what teachers are or necessarily should be focused on, which counters the Negative's argument that teachers are focused on promoting corporate social responsibility.

Rhetorical questions that imply the answer.

But perhaps some power to influence is superior to having no power at all.

If teachers want to help children and society beyond academics, what exactly is wrong with that?

For these reasons, we stand proudly in favor of this important resolution, and I would be pleased to answer any questions or criticism in the cross-examination.

First Negative: Let's talk about the concept of program funding. Would it be fair to say that the more money a school has, the more able it is to provide enhancing activities, such as field trips and special events?

Clear 'signpost' of the cross-examiner's purpose.

Second Affirmative: Well, yes, but not if it negatively impacts the school environment.

Links back to the 'yardstick' to measure suitability.

First Negative: Is it also fair to say that every school has different needs in this regard?

Second Affirmative: Yes.

Obvious answer to obvious question.

First Negative: So, if a school wants to pursue a unique activity, would corporate sponsorships not help them achieve this goal?

Second Affirmative: Perhaps, but don't forget the significant harm it imposes on the school learning environment.

Speaker refusing to play into the cross-examiner's hands.

First Negative: I see. So you are admitting, then, that without the sponsorship, the school may not be able to pursue these value-added initiatives?

Trying again a second time, good to persist this way.

Second Affirmative: No, not at all. There are other ways to raise funds, such as involving parents and students, or seeking grants from the government or non-profit groups.

Standing firm, and enhancing the previous answer.

First Affirmative: Thank you, it seems that our time has expired.

Chairperson: I thank the second speaker of the Affirmative, and now call upon the second speaker of the Negative to conclude the constructive part of the debate.

Second Negative: Ladies and gentlemen, let me get right into the new constructive arguments brought up by the second speaker of the Affirmative team. He started by talking about how kids are vulnerable to advertisements. Ultimately, though, it is the responsibility of parents to teach their kids about making responsible choices. As I will tell you about later, corporations will find a way to reach kids anyway. This debate is not about whether corporate advertising to students is good or bad. It is about whether schools specifically are harmed by this practice. Certainly, this point would be interesting in the context of a wider debate about advertising to children, but it does not show you that advertising in a school environment creates additional harms. We believe that a student certainly knows the difference between an advertisement and a learning point.

Quite general, but perhaps there's no time to waste here.

Clear distinction, but are parents around to help during the day?

Explains effectively what the real issue is.

Can a young student make such as distinction so easily?

Next, the second Affirmative speaker claimed that corporate sponsorship distracts away from learning. The reality, however, is that the vast majority of corporate sponsorship takes place outside of a class. It is tough to make the argument that a gymnasium named after a company, a poster on a wall, or the products in a vending machine distracts from what students learn in their courses. Even though the primary purpose of a school is learning, during breaks, at lunch, and before and after school, learning is clearly not the focus of attention. As for classroom activities, is there anything essentially wrong with the product being promoted, so long as the students are learning an important concept at the same time?

A well-stated point that most people would agree is true.

But isn't the environment still important?

A risky statement, probably best to explain further.

At this point, we would like to introduce the final two points of the Negative case. These arguments focus on the idea that advertising within a school is a beneficial advantage over the advertising that would take place outside of the school. Our third point is that if corporations are going to spend money advertising to kids anyways, at least having a company sponsoring school provides some benefit to society. In the process of meeting its commercial objectives, a business is also improving the education of students through its funding. Alternatively, it would have simply spent these advertising dollars by paying, for example, television companies. Therefore, there is more value created to society through this win-win arrangement.

Clear statement of overall theme.

Spin-off benefits of the inevitable.

Opposes directly the Affirmative's concept of value.

Our fourth and final point is that advertising within a school takes place within a filtered, sheltered environment. The Affirmative has talked about how advertising in schools makes it more difficult for parents to raise their kids as they wish. In reality, students see advertisements in many places, from billboards and posters to television and radio commercials, almost completely unfiltered by parents. At least in a school, officials have the ability to screen out advertisements and sponsorships that they believe are inappropriate. Additionally, it's more likely that there will be a fair critique and evaluation of advertisements by teachers and students within the school. Clearly, a school provides a less harmful environment for corporate sponsorship than in the world outside of school.

So why should we accept even more advertising?

If a company is paying money, what interest is there to screen? Who would critique them, and why would they bother?

These two points, combined with my partner's points about funding for programs and the influence that schools can have on corporate activities, provide a solid case in favor of corporate sponsorship in schools. I have shown you that the Affirmative's third and fourth points about the vulnerability of kids and the distraction to learning do not support their side of this round's resolution. Therefore, this resolution must fall, and I now stand open for cross-examination.

Good wrap-up of the speech and the case, lays the ground for the rebuttal.

Second Affirmative: I want to talk about your idea of a school as some type of filtered environment. If a company was helping pay for new music equipment, do you agree that a school would be less likely to screen out the sponsor's advertisement?

Statement of purpose.

Specific example makes the concept more tangible.

Second Negative: Well, at least the school can make an informed choice over who should sponsor the purchases and what the corporation is allowed to do in exchange.

What does "informed choice" mean in terms of outcomes?

Second Affirmative: But this sponsoring company, couldn't it simply go to another school if this particular school decides to be picky?

Suggests how the company has more power than the school

Second Negative: I suppose so, yes.

Qualify this answer.

Second Affirmative: So then the school would be without any additional funding support for its music program?

Statement of harms.

Second Negative: No, it would simply have to look elsewhere for a sponsor that did not compromise the learning environment.

Good answer, rejects harms and supports am important pillar of the Negative's case.

Second Affirmative: You also mentioned critiquing and evaluating sponsorships and advertisements. So, if a company has its name placed over the school gymnasium, do you see students and teachers walking by and saying to each other, "Let's do an analysis of this company's intent and practices?"

Is this a new issue or a continuation of the existing one?

This scenario helps to illustrate.

Second Negative: I think you're trivializing the issue. At least when a company makes a questionable claim, a school is a place where debate takes place. Certainly more so than when someone is driving by a billboard or watching television.

It would be tough to answer the question directly in this case.

Second Affirmative: Thank you, our cross-examination time has finished.

Chairperson: I thank the second speaker of the Negative for her remarks. We now move into the rebuttal phase. I would like to remind the debaters that no new contentions can be made during this time. I now call upon the first speaker of the Negative team to deliver the Negative rebuttal.

First Negative: Today's debate has centered on two competing themes. The first theme was the impact of corporate sponsorship on the operation of schools. The second theme,

Good idea to state the central themes from the outset.

discussed mainly by the second speaker of each team, was about the impact of corporate sponsorship in schools on students. In my rebuttal, I will show you why the Negative team has prevailed on both of these core themes.

Helps the judges to see the 'big picture' of the debate and how it fits with the structure.

The Affirmative's case on the school operation theme made a number of unfounded assumptions. It assumed that corporate sponsorship compromises the objective of administrators to consider the best interest of students, when in fact the mandate and evaluation of schools is based on the overall quality of student education. It also falsely assumed that corporate sponsorship necessarily meant less government funding, when in fact the accountability of the government to provide quality education and basic funding for core programs demonstrates the flaws in this argument. We showed you how corporate sponsorship actually benefits schools, both in terms of funding for value added programs and the ability of schools to influence corporate activities that relate to their objectives. The Affirmative failed to show you what would make up for these benefits if not for corporate sponsorship.

Outlines the way in which the Affirmative's case is flawed.

Refutes while raising a constructive point.

A second instance of an assumption, strengthens the claim.

Draws a contrast, "We showed you" vs. "The Affirmative failed."

The Affirmative case on the student impact theme also rested on several unproven assumptions. It assumed that schools can somehow decrease the vulnerability of students to corporate influence, when in reality students are influenced by advertising anywhere they see it and ultimately, parents are responsible for teaching their kids how to make good choices. It assumed that corporate sponsorship distracts attention away from learning, when in reality it typically takes place outside of the classroom or does not take away from the learning experience. We showed you that if corporations are go-

Continues with false assumptions method.

A fairly long-winded passage.

Would be helpful to clarify or explain this concept further.

ing to advertise to kids anyways, doing so in a school has a positive spin-off for education and takes place in a more filtered environment. The Affirmative essentially focused on corporate advertising in general, as opposed to why it would be any worse in schools.

Claims why the Affirmative's approach was flawed.

Since we have clearly demonstrated how the Negative has won the debate on the school operations theme and the student impact theme, we rest our case.

Brings back and reinforces the themes one more time.

Chairperson: I would now like to call upon the first speaker of the Affirmative team to conclude today's debate.

First Affirmative: In deciding which team won the debate, we argue that there are two central questions: what is the purpose of a school, and does corporate sponsorship fit within this purpose? Today, we have demonstrated that corporate sponsorship and the objectives of a school are fundamentally incompatible.

Phrasing the issues as questions encourages the judges to see them as the key criteria.

Let me begin by talking about the purpose of a school. We have talked about how administrators should focus solely on the interests of students. We have also discussed how students should be in school to focus on learning. A school, in our view, it essentially different than the world around it, and that it is supposed to present an environment suitable for student development.

Summary of underlying points of the Affirmative's case.

But where is the refutation?

Now, let me explore whether corporate advertising fits within this mandate. We have demonstrated how administrators have to balance student interests with corporate interests when sponsorships are taking place. The Negative naïvely and incorrectly argued that schools will supposedly influence corporations and effectively screen advertisements. This, however, is neither the goal,

Explain how it's been demonstrated.

nor the core capability of a school. We have shown you how corporate sponsorship in schools exploits the vulnerability of kids and distracts them away from learning. The Negative would have you believe that this is somehow better than in the outside world. We could not disagree more. Leave corporate advertising, which has nothing to do with the education of children, to the outside world.

Clear rejection of the Negative's claims.

Draws a contrast.

We have proven on every dimension of this debate that corporate sponsorship is completely out of place when it comes to school objectives and student learning. Therefore, the corporate sponsorship of schools does far more harm than any good. Thank you.

Concludes the rebuttal fairly quickly, more depth would have been helpful.

Chairperson: I now declare that this debate has concluded. I invite the debaters to cross the floor and to shake hands.

COMMENTARY ON "SPONSORSHIP" DEBATE

The debate has clear-cut, contentious issues, and both teams articulated a number of relevant points on these issues. In some cases, the explanations and support for these points could have gone further. The cross-examination periods were lively, with the questioners asking tough, targeted questions.

What did the Affirmative do well?

• *Perspectives on the role of a school.* The Affirmative made the principle of a school being exclusively for learning a central part of its case. This principle was used effectively to suggest how corporate sponsorships violate this principle.

• *Discussion of impact on decision-makers.* Both speakers did a good job of explaining how corporate sponsorship places administrators and teachers in a conflict of interest situation, having to balance student learning with financial matters. This practical analysis added to the principle of what a school should and should not be.

• *Analysis of a child's vulnerability.* The examination of how a child's mind operates was important in backing up the Affirmative's claim that the advertising had a negative influence. Many debaters could have complicated this type of analysis, whereas the Affirmative team made it easy to understand.

What could the Affirmative have improved?

• *Impact of lost revenues on schools.* Since it's widely accepted that less funding for schools isn't desirable, the Affirmative team should have explained further how the benefits of stopping corporate sponsorship clearly outweighed the costs. Would certain program have to be stopped and, if so, was it worthwhile considering the stated improvements to the school?

• *Rebuttal had insufficient explanation and depth.* While the speaker did frame the key issues effectively, the discussion that followed wasn't thorough enough to demonstrate clearly how the Affirmative came ahead on the criteria presented. On a number of points, there was no refutation of the Negative's points, only a broad summary of the Affirmative's arguments.

What did the Negative do well?

• *Comments on positive impact of corporate sponsorships.* While the argument that additional funding is helpful may seem like an obvious one, the Negative team explained specifically how it benefits the schools. The discussion on enhancements to schools, such as field trips and music programs, illustrated what they stand to lose if there are no corporate sponsorships.

• *Opposition to the harms presented by the Affirmative.* Although it was tough to refute this point in every respect, the Negative did explain how in many cases corporate sponsorship doesn't necessarily have a negative impact. For example, the naming of a school gymnasium was cited appropriately as a win-win arrangement.

• *Attack of the Affirmative's case in the rebuttal.* The first Negative speaker's rebuttal was highly structured around core themes, and on each theme there was clear and direct refutation of the Affirmative's arguments and assumptions. The comparisons made with the Negative's case enhanced the refutation.

What could the Negative have improved?

• *Argument on comparative advantages of school advertising.* The second Negative speaker wasn't entirely convincing in arguing that schools could "filter" advertisements and that the supposedly "sheltered" environment made sponsorships acceptable. It wasn't clear how this would happen, or why the school environment would make the advertising any less influential on children.

• *Answers to cross-examination questions.* The first Negative speaker should have been more thorough and direct in answering the cross-examiner's questions. Several of the answers were more quips aimed at quickly rebuffing the cross-examiner, rather than more thorough defenses of the Negative's case.

SPONSORSHIP DEBATE: FLOW SHEET

AFFIRMATIVE	NEGATIVE
1st Affirmative (#1)	**1st Negative (#2)**
Definition: Any marketing in schools, Freedonia School District	
1. Administrator conflict of interest	Clash 1: Primary focus is learning
2. Relationship with government	Clash 2: Only for enhancement
2nd Affirmative (#3)	
Clash 1: Costs to learning outweigh	1. Valuable funding to schools
Clash 2: Greater corporate influence	2. Some impact on corporations
	2nd Negative (#4)
3. Kids are vulnerable to advertising	Clash 3: Parent responsibility
4. Distracts attention from learning	Clash 4: Usually not in class
1st Affirmative (#6)	
	3. Win-win arrangement for society
	4. Filtered, sheltered environment
	1st Negative (#5)
Question 1: What is the purpose of a school? Interests of students and their learning comes first, an environment that is a departure from the outside world.	Theme 1: Impact of corporate sponsorship on administration of schools. Affirmative made unfounded assumptions, Negative showed how there are benefits.
Question 2: Does corporate sponsorship fit within this purpose? Takes away from student learning environment, let advertising stay in the outside world.	Theme 2: Impact of corporate sponsorship on students. Affirmative made unfounded assumptions, Negative proved that there are positive spin-offs.

Chapter 12: Keys to Success

✔ **Notice how a speaker identifies specifically which point he or she is refuting**. This makes it much easier for the judges to keep track of how well you are clashing. Either in their minds or on paper, they can 'check off' each point as it is opposed.

✔ **Observe how the strongest debaters had a clear overall speech structure**. They told the audience exactly where they were going, they followed this road map, and they finished by reminding everyone about what they have said. This served to reinforce the key messages.

✔ **Take note of the importance that persistence plays in a cross-examination**. The cross-examiner stuck to a particular line of questioning, rather than being side-tracked by the responses. But the person answering the questions was sure to explain the answers to avoid seeming weakened and to prevent the cross-examiner from extracting the desired answers.

✔ **Recognize how the rebuttal speakers brought the debate down to one or two issues**. You didn't see minor arguments or evidence brought up in the rebuttals. For the Negative or Opposition, it was helpful to put the opponent on the defensive by stating clearly what the main questions or themes were.

Conclusion
The Will to Win with Ethics and Respect

It's no accident that I've written this book largely in the third-person. My primary goal wasn't to infuse the text with my personal opinions. Rather, my intent was to present useful information compiled from many sources and learned from many people.

Allow me, then, to depart briefly from this objectivity and to use this space for some personal thoughts. Firstly, I want to discuss what it means to have the will to win at the sport of debate. Secondly, I hope to get across the vital role that honesty and respect play in debate. Finally, I want to talk about the vital role that debate plays in making the world 'tick'.

THE QUEST FOR VICTORY

Debate tournaments can be very competitive. They place intelligent, well-spoken people who believe passionately that they're right in direct opposition to one another. Don't view this competition as a barrier. Instead, you should thrive on healthy rivalry and allow it to motivate you to excel. Never get discouraged if you don't always place as well as you had hoped. Never give up. If you believe in yourself and persist in achieving your personal best, you'll improve your performance and reach the medal podium.

This competitive environment extends well beyond tournaments. Any 'real world' debate involves, by its very nature, some level of rivalry. Everyone wants to win the argument, both to achieve their objectives and to feel personal satisfaction. Unfortunately, you'll rarely get everything you want, so be prepared to work with others. The will to win may involve sacrificing what's least important to you but valued by others, so that you can achieve what's most important to you and nonessential to your peers. In many cases, having the will to win means helping the *team* win, rather than aiming for a *personal* victory at the expense of others participants.

THE ETHICS OF ENGAGEMENT

It's critically important that you maintain your ethics in any competitive debate environment. Never make up evidence or misrepresent yourself, even if you may get away with it a few times. Not only will you be cheating yourself, but you'll eventually get a reputation for playing against the rules. Although you're welcome to be assertive, make sure that you're courteous to your opponents. Respect the judges, coaches, parents, and volunteers who help run debate workshops and tournaments. The experience of competition should be enjoyable. Don't allow it to become tense and disrespectful.

Similar principles apply when you debate in daily situations. If you're ethical and respectful, your arguments will have much more impact. Other people will want to listen to what you have to say. The skills of debating should help you become more influential when decisions are made, but they shouldn't be used to insult or diminish the contributions made by other participants.

DEBATE AS A DRIVER OF DECISIONS

It's my conviction that debate is a vital part of the world around us. I believe that the best ideas emerge from vigorous debate. The best ideas emerge in the classroom when students speak freely and confidently about what they're learning. The best ideas emerge in companies when team members debate the decisions they face thoroughly and intelligently. The best ideas emerge in society when there's lively debate within government, in the media, and among the citizenry.

Debate can and should play a central role in how you contribute to society. More than ever before, 'thought leaders' have come to the forefront of how the world operates. You can use the power of persuasion to contribute to the democratic life of your country, or to contribute to the advancement of a worthy cause. It's up to you how you use the skills of debate, but know that you possess the ability to use it to improve the world around you.

AND NOW, IT'S UP TO YOU!

I hope that this book has provided you with a solid base of information about the art of speech and debate. Now, it's up to you to put this information into action. It will take time and effort, and you will get frustrated. But if you have the will to excel, you will do so. I have benefited a great deal from speech and debate, and it's become part of everything I do. I hope that *Talk the Talk* will play at least a small role in helping you do the same.

As you embark on your own road to victory, you're welcome and encouraged to write to me with your questions, observations, criticisms, suggestions, or anything else that's on your mind. Whether you're a competitive debater, a debate coach, or even a parent who wants either to thank or scold me for helping turn your dinner table into a debate forum, I look forward to reading (and responding to) what you have to say.

Alim Merali
alim@talkthetalk.ca
www.talkthetalk.ca

DEBATER'S RULE #1

"I am always right."

DEBATER'S RULE #2

"If you think I am wrong, see Rule #1."

Appendix A
Debate Resolutions

Preliminary phrases such as "This House would" (THW), "This House believes that" (THBT), "Be it resolved that" (BIRT), or "Resolved:" come before a debate resolution. The first two are seen mostly in parliamentary style debate, "THW" implying a policy debate and "THBT" signaling a values debate. The last two are found in academic, discussion, and cross-examination styles.

As you read each of the resolutions, think about the type of debate it suggests. Is it a values debate involving competing principles? Or is it a policy debate involving a set of needs for change and a plan of action? In some cases, you'll find that the resolution can be spun into either a values debate or a policy debate.

Think also about the variety of issues that could fall under each resolution. Debating multiple areas is usually beyond the scope of one round. You may find it necessary to narrow the resolution so that a more focused debate can take place. You're also encouraged to modify, flip around, or come up with a spin-off of the resolution to create the type of debate you want.

SPORTS

Commercialization has improved the Olympics.
Professional boxing should be banned.
Sports teams should be held responsible for mischief by their fans.
Women's and men's sports teams should receive equal support.
International sport has a place in international politics.
Professional athletes are paid too much.
Sports entertainment should not be considered sport.

EDUCATION

School uniforms limit diversity and creativity.
Standardized tests should be eliminated.
Single-sex schools are preferable to co-ed schools.
Students learn more from their peers than from their teachers.
Private schools should receive government funding.
The school discipline system needs reforming.
Year-round schooling should be implemented.
Students should have a say in how schools are run.
There is too much emphasis on marks.
Post-secondary education should be publicly-funded.
The government should subsidize foreign educational experiences.
Home-schooling is an acceptable alternative to traditional schools.
Learning a second language should be mandatory.
Parents should play a major role in the operation of schools.

CULTURE

Museums and theatres should fund themselves.
Hollywood has negatively influenced our culture.
Minority language rights are worth protecting.
Foreign cultural influences should be restricted.
The government should censor the arts.

SOCIAL

Parenting lessons should be mandatory.
Life has become too competitive.
The people are not as tolerant as they think they are.
Celebrities should also be role models.
The advertising of alcohol should be banned.
The feminist movement has failed.
Private groups should not have the right to discriminate.
Children should never be spanked.

MEDIA

Journalists should not use confidential sources.
The entertainment media has a negative influence.
The more free the press, the more free the people.
All broadcasters should be private organizations.
The media has a social responsibility.
The number of television advertising minutes should be limited.
Restrictions should be placed on video game violence.
The government should impose domestic content requirements.

TECHNOLOGY

The government should regulate Internet content.
There should be a fee for each e-mail sent.
Internet 'blogs' are legitimate journalism.
Internet chat is harming our young generation.
Technology has gone too far.
Computer technology can solve our problems.

SCIENCE

Space exploration is a waste of time and money.
Scientific research should be available for public use.
Space tourism is a worthwhile objective.
Genetic engineering has a positive impact.
The patenting of pharmaceuticals should be ended.
The government should not fund commercial science.

DEMOCRACY

Dictatorship is preferable to anarchy.
A noble dictator is superior to a selfish democrat.
Police and intelligence powers should be limited.
Public security is more important than individual rights.
Prisoners should have the right to vote.
Children should not have a right to privacy.
Hate speech should not be considered free speech.

Citizens should be allowed to initiate binding referenda.
Medical professionals should have the right to strike.
Civil disobedience is a legitimate expression of democratic will.
Individuals have too many rights and freedoms.
The minimum voting age should be lowered.

POLITICS

Publicly-funded healthcare is a human right.
The business of government is business.
A national identity card should be implemented.
Campaign funding should be more strictly regulated.
The present government should compensate victims of past abuses.

ECONOMY

Progressive taxes should be replaced by single-rate taxes.
Farmers and ranchers should receive subsidies.
The national debt should be paid off faster.
Public corporations should be privatized.
The rich pay too much tax.
The minimum wage should be abolished.

ENVIRONMENT

Global warming is the enemy.
Capitalism and environmentalism cannot co-exist.
National parks should be protected against tourism.
Recreational fishing and hunting should be prohibited.
Recycling should be mandatory.
Endangered species should be protected.

INTERNATIONAL

Multilateralism is preferable to unilateralism.
The threat of force is the best way to create peace.
There should be a 'Marshall Plan' for Africa.
A 'strike first' policy should be used to confront enemies.

The United Nations should have a military.
The United Nations has been a failure.
The testing of nuclear weapons should be banned.
Following orders is no excuse for committing war crimes.
Stable dictatorships are preferable to unstable democracies.
Universal human rights do not exist.
Political assassinations are justified acts of war.

LAW

The death penalty is cruel and unusual punishment.
Punishment is more important than rehabilitation.
Criminals have too many rights and freedoms.
Torture is never justified.
Let a hundred guilty go free if it saves one innocent.
Jury duty should be optional.
Criminals should serve their full sentences.
Court trials should be televised.
Illegal immigrants should receive criminal treatment.
Judges have a role to play as social activists.
Criminal trials should be decided by a judge alone.
The justice system is too soft on criminal activity.
Drunk drivers should be banned from driving permanently.
Criminals should not be allowed to profit while in prison.
Young offenders should be tried as adults.
An unjust law should be broken.
The law should protect people from themselves.
Driving while talking on a cell phone should be illegal.

GENERAL

People should obey rules over their consciences.
Individuals have no impact on the world.
The entrepreneur is more important than the artist.
It is preferable to be right than to be successful.
Chance has a greater role than choice.
Conviction is more honorable than consensus.
Authority should always be questioned.
The family is more important than the government.

Leaders are responsible for the actions of their teams.
Knowledge is gained through experience.

OPEN

Open debate resolutions shouldn't be taken literally. If they are, they're bound to be abstract beyond tangible debate. This type of resolution requires the Affirmative team to link the resolution to a more concrete issue, which allows it to present virtually any case that it wants. The Negative team must respond based on the definition presented, making it next to impossible to prepare for the debate in advance.

Wag the dog until the wolves come out.
The pen is mightier than the sword.
The egg came before the chicken.
The Yankees deserve respect.
McDonald's is the way of the future.
The cow should be milked dry.
Apples should not be compared to oranges.
There is no black and white, only shades of grey.
Silver is good, but gold is great.
Roses are red, violets are blue.
It's music to the ears and food to the soul.
The chicken has to cross the road.
The right to be wrong is a right.
Good fences make good neighbors.
The end is within reach.

Appendix B
Judging Criteria

The set of criteria used to evaluate debaters depends on the region, level, and style of debate. Even if the criteria are similar, the total number of points, the weight placed on each area, and the scoring guidelines may vary significantly. In general, a judge has two responsibilities: assign scores to each speaker and decide which team won the debate. This section explores some of the questions judges usually ask themselves when evaluating a debate.

These criteria also serve as a useful summary and reminder of many of the book's most important concepts. When you prepare to debate and as you continually evaluate your performance, think about how you're measuring up on these dimensions. You want your judges to be able to put a 'check mark' beside each of the questions.

INDIVIDUAL SCORE

When evaluating you individually, judges are thinking about how well you contributed to the overall dynamic of the debate. Did the *matter* you presented—arguments and refutation—add value to the debate? And did the *manner* in which you presented it—organization and delivery—make you an effective, compelling speaker? There are usually five categories that a judge considers: *Content*, *Refutation*, *Organization*, *Delivery*, and *Procedure*.

Content (5 points)

• **Themes**. Did the debater's arguments center around a single theme or a closely related set of themes? Were the themes selected appropriate and clearly presented? The wise use of central themes provides a sense of coherency to the case. It allows the debate to come down to a core group of key ideas.

• **Arguments**. How strong were the arguments used to support the overall themes? Was it easy for you to understand each argument and to describe it with a short phrase? Carefully selected arguments instantly provide a sense of strength to the debater's case.

• **Explanations**. Did the speaker use sound explanations and logic to expand on the arguments? How well did the explanations cover the key dimensions of each point? The debater should go beyond stating an argument and expecting you to agree with it. His or her explanation should strengthen the point against any possible attacks.

• **Evidence**. Was sufficient evidence and example employed to support the explanations? Was the backup presented effective and relevant to the argument it was intended to enhance? If any of the debater's claims are questionable or unclear, you should expect them to be supported. It should also be made very clear to you how the evidence proves the argument in question.

Refutation (5 points)

• **Completeness**. Was the clash complete, covering every relevant point of the opposing team's case? The debater shouldn't leave any of the opposing team's key points untouched. As you track the debate on your flow sheet, check off each argument that the debater has refuted.

• **Prioritization**. Did the clash focus on the most important areas of the other team's case? There's no requirement that a debater spend equal time refuting each argument. The debater should be able to distinguish between the other team's central and less important points, adjusting his or her emphasis accordingly.

• **Effectiveness**. Was the clash successful at exposing flaws in the opponent's arguments? The refutation of each point should be thorough enough to raise serious doubts. It should hit on the key weaknesses and explain persuasively why each argument is wrong.

Organization (5 points)

• **Introduction**. Did the introduction effectively lay out the core themes and direction of the team's case? The way a debater begins should prepare you for what's to come. He or she should compel you to listen to the forthcoming material.

• **Conclusion**. Did the conclusion bring the case together and wrap it up in a way that made it understandable? A conclusion, while short, should hit on the key issues and outcomes of the debater's speech.

• **Structure**. Was there a clear structure that broke the case down into clear and logical parts? Did the order in which the points were presented make sense? The way a debater structures a case should make it easy for you to follow and take notes.

• **Flow**. Within each point, did the speaker have a clear and logical flow? This doesn't mean that the debater is required to provide obvious 'signposts' within each point. However, as the debater moves through the point, the flow should seem smooth and effective.

• **Transitions**. When moving between points, were there smooth transitions? Did they make it clear what the speaker had just accomplished and where he or she was going next? Excellent transitions guide you through the speech, helping tie together the distinct points.

Delivery (5 points)

• **Eye Contact**. Did the speaker maintain strong eye contact with the entire audience? The debater's eye contact should convey confidence and engagement. You shouldn't see the debater spending most of his or her speaking time reading text from a page.

• **Pace**. Was the speaking speed appropriate for the audience? Did it allow everyone to understand clearly the points being made? This doesn't mean that the debater has to talk at the same rate throughout the entire speech, as variety can add character and liveliness.

• **Posture**. Did the speaker maintain strong posture and presence? Like solid eye contact, good posture and body movement make a debater appear more confident and engaging.

• **Clarity**. How clearly did the speaker articulate the content? Was it easy to understand what he or she was saying? While it certainly isn't necessary to articulate every single syllable robotically, the words and phrases shouldn't seem mumbled or slurred.

• **Expression**. How dynamic was the speaker's delivery? Did the debater vary his or her pitch and volume appropriately? This really comes down to your overall impression. Think about how interested you were as the debater spoke.

• **Gestures**. Were hand gestures used effectively to add meaning to the delivery? Hand gestures should flow naturally according to the debater's style. It's important that they don't seem repetitive, but they shouldn't be flashy to the point of distraction.

Procedure (5 points)

• **Process**. Did the debater follow the correct procedure for the style of debate? Were the time limits observed? Were the other debaters, the judges, and the moderator addressed appropriately? While these factors don't impact the substantive part of the debate, they do speak to the debater's respect for the rules and traditions of competition.

• **Courtesy**. Was the debater respectful and courteous to everyone in the room? Did he or she avoid making personal attacks or derogatory comments? There's nothing wrong with a debater being assertive, even aggressive. But above all, the competitor should be making a positive contribution to the experience of everyone in the room.

• **Questions**. Did the debater ask strong, targeted questions to challenge the opponent's points? Were the questions relevant to the issue at hand? This applies to Points of Information in parliamentary debate, the question period in discussion debate, and after each constructive speech in cross-examination debate.

• **Answers**. How effectively and completely did the debater answer the other team's questions? Did he or she appear confident and fluent when providing the answers? If the answers were in response to a Point of Information in parliamentary debate, did the debater transition back to the speech in a smooth way? The competitor has to strike a good balance between answering the question fully and not appearing to be on the defensive.

Total Score (25 points)

Judges are often asked to follow scoring ranges, which are targets prescribed by tournament directors to ensure consistent evaluations from room to room. A typical guide for a total score out of 25 points is to stick within a range of 15 to 23 points. This would result in an average score of 19 points, plus or minus one point depending on the overall strength of debate in the room. Some judges prefer to use the specific criteria discussed previously to arrive at a score, whereas others use them only as a guidelines to reach a total score. Here are descriptions of the different levels:

<15 points. Rarely should a debater receive a score this low. A score under 15 points indicates that the debater didn't fulfill his or her role in the debate. The speech was incomplete and virtually impossible for any reasonable person to follow.

15 to 17 points. Some debaters, particularly beginners, may fall within this scoring range. There was clearly preparation and thought put into the case. Unfortunately, significant errors and shortcomings hurt the overall effectiveness.

17 to 19 points. A score within this range is considered average. The debater presented arguments reasonably well. He or she clashed with the other team's points, but may not have been thorough enough in many places. The style was adequate and the structure was fairly clear, but neither element was exceptional.

20 to 22 points. This score indicates an excellent performance. The debater presented arguments, clashed with the other team's points, and articulated the case in a confident, organized, and effective manner. He or she clearly stood out in the round.

23 points. A score this high should be reserved for a top-notch performance. There should probably be only a handful in the tournament, the recipients of which would almost certainly be contenders for the top speaker awards. To earn this score, every aspect of debate has to be done exceptionally well.

24 points. You're falling off your chair because you've been dazzled beyond your wildest expectations. You would pay money to see this person debate again, or even for an autograph.

25 points. The debater is perfect. Superhuman, actually.

TEAM DECISION

Usually, the team with the higher speaking score between the two debaters wins the debate. Doesn't it make sense that the debaters with stronger arguments and more effective refutation should win? In the vast majority of cases, this is true. But there are some debate tournaments that allow 'low point wins'. This means that a team could have been less proficient in its debating skills, such as style and procedure, but still have won the overall argument. There are two questions that a judge should ask in deciding who won the debate, both of them different ways of stating a similar measuring stick:

• **Trial test**. If you were a judge in a trial on this issue and had to decide objectively which team made a stronger case with its arguments and refutation, who would you select? Or, if you were randomly assigned to either side in a courtroom battle on this resolution, which team would you want to be your legal counsel?

• **Burden test**. Which team did a more effective job at meeting its burden in the debate? That is, which one was more successful at fulfilling its obligations according to the definitions presented and your interpretation of each team's responsibilities?

Glossary

You were promised a book light on technical jargon. Hopefully, this promise has been fulfilled. The book did, however, present a number of uncomplicated and easy to learn terms that are part of the speech and debate lexicon. This glossary is designed to give you a quick reference and a short refresher on many of these expressions.

Academic debate: The most basic form of debate. There are normally four constructive speeches between the two teams, as well as two rebuttal speeches. In this style, there are no opportunities for debaters to ask critical questions to one another.

Affirmative: The team that argues for the resolution in academic, discussion, and cross-examination styles of debate. Opens and usually closes the debate. Sometimes called the Proposition team.

Argument: A single, specific idea presented to build a team's case, generally possible to summarize in one sentence. Each team should have between four and six individual arguments in its case. May also be called a contention or a point.

Bill: An alternative name for the resolution in a parliamentary debate. Parliaments pass laws called Bills, and the use of this term is intended to match this practice.

BIRT: Short for the phrase, "Be it resolved that." Often placed before the resolution in academic, discussion, and cross-examination debates.

Body language: The way that a speaker uses posture, movement, gestures, and expression to project a strong visual impression.

Burden: The extent to which each team has to prove its case for or against the resolution. Usually, the Affirmative team has a slightly greater burden, because it defines the terms. The degree of burden may also depend on the relative difficulty of each side.

Case: The set of arguments, explanations, and evidence presented for or against a resolution. Usually consists of one or two central themes, each supported by multiple points.

Clash: Countering the opponent's case point by point. This type of specific, targeted refutation takes place mostly in the constructive speeches, leaving the rebuttal speeches for more general criticism of the other team's arguments.

Constructive speech: A speech that involves new constructive arguments, defense of previous constructive arguments, and refutation of the opponent's case. Normally, the first four speeches of a debate, or two by each team, are the constructive speeches.

Counter plan: A Negative team case strategy that involves agreeing with the needs for change, but proposing a substantially different plan to solve the problem.

Criteria: A set of objectives that a system must meet in order to be judged effective or appropriate. Criteria are sometimes used by the Affirmative team to frame the debate in a way it considers favorable.

Cross-examination debate: A style of debate that involves questioning of a speaker by someone from the opposing team to highlight weaknesses or to attain admissions. A cross-examination, usually three to four minutes long, takes place following each constructive speech.

Definition: Clarification and interpretation of the resolution's terms by the first speaker of the Affirmative team. Definitions may be used to narrow a broad debate to a more focused subject. Both teams must abide by the definitions throughout the round.

Discussion debate: A debate style that includes a discussion period, up to 10 minutes long, between the constructive part of the debate and the beginning of the rebuttal speeches. Teams take turns asking critical questions to each other.

Flow sheet: A columned sheet used to keep track of each speaker's arguments and refutation. Arrows are often drawn between each argument and the matching clash to help visualize the back and forth flow of the debate. Used by both judges and competitors.

Government: The team arguing for the Bill in a parliamentary debate. The Prime Minister (P.M.) opens the debate with a constructive speech and ends the debate with a rebuttal speech. The Minister of the Crown (M.C.) speaks in between the Prime Minister's speeches.

Heckle: A short, witty, and to the point interjection in parliamentary debate. Heckles, which are usually humorous, should be not be questions or arguments. They are best restricted to no more than five words, and then so only used occasionally, if at all.

House: The chamber or room where a parliamentary debate takes place. There are specific rules and traditions of the House that the debaters must follow.

Impromptu speaking: Communicating with limited or no notes, either spontaneously or with minimal preparation. Impromptu speaking is used in a variety of situations, such as debate rounds, questions after a speech, and class or committee discussions.

Informative speech: A speech to explain or clarify an issue or to provide instruction on a process. An informative speech is based heavily on factual information and requires, in particular, clear descriptions.

Leading questions: Questions that imply or push for the desired answer. This is the most effective type of question to ask in a cross-examination. Usually starts with phrases like "Would you acknowledge that …" or "Isn't it true that …"

Memorized speaking: Presenting a speech word for word without any notes. While this method can be very time-consuming and, for most people, makes it tough to seem natural, it may be useful to memorize key parts of a speech.

Model Parliament: A simulation of a political debate in which participants represent different political parties in a legislature. The members debate and vote on Bills to be passed into law. In the United States, this type of forum is generally known as Student Congress.

Model United Nations: A type of forum debate in which participants each represent countries on a United Nations committee, such as the Security Council or a General Assembly. The debates take place on resolutions that are put forth by member states.

Needs-plan-benefits: A type of Affirmative team case in a policy debate involving reasons to change the present system, plans for implementing the stated changes, and anticipated benefits of the proposed reforms. Tells the judges "why, what, and so what" in support of the resolution.

Negative: The team that argues against the resolution in academic, discussion, and cross-examination styles of debate. Although the Negative team has some flexibility in how it makes its case, it's arguments must fit with the definitions presented by the Affirmative team.

Opposition: The team opposing the Bill in a parliamentary debate. The Member of the Opposition (M.O.) begins the Opposition's case. The Leader of the Opposition (L.O.) speaks second and divides his or her speech into constructive time and rebuttal time.

Outline speaking: Speech delivery using a short list of ideas, allowing for maximum engagement with the audience. The most basic form of outline speaking is a list of the speech's main points, but some speakers prefer to include sub-points as well.

Parliamentary debate: A style based in part on the traditions of legislatures around the world. In addition to formal terms and rules, it features different types of interjections, such as Points of Information, Points of Order, Points of Personal Privilege, and heckles.

Persuasive speech: A speech intended to convince the audience of a perspective or of the need to take action on an issue. Although it's supported by factual information, persuading the audience members with sound logic and both rational and emotional appeals is central to the speaker's approach.

Plan: A set of policy proposals brought forth by the Affirmative team to meet its stated needs for change. A plan outlines the numerous steps that the agents of change must take in order to address the present system's shortcomings in an effective and feasible way.

Point of Information: A brief, challenging question during an opponent's constructive speech in parliamentary debate. The person who has the floor may decide either to accept or reject a Point of Information request as the opposing debater rises.

Point of Order: An accusation that a debater has broken a rule of parliamentary debate, judged by the Speaker as "well taken" or "not well taken." Not recommended for exposing frivolous violations, such as placing hands in one's pockets or holding a pen.

Policy debate: A debate involving a plan that addresses the Affirmative's stated needs for change. The debate usually focuses on two dimensions, namely whether change is necessary and, if so, whether the Affirmative's plan is desirable.

Qualification: Providing an explanation when answering the cross-examiner's "yes or no" question. Qualifying an answer allows the speaker to defend his or her case more effectively. However, the qualification should not be so lengthy that it seems like a speech.

Rebuttal: The final speech of the debate by each team. Each rebuttal speaker aims to bring the debate down to key themes and underlying principles, and to suggest to the judges what the deciding issues are. Both refutation of the opposing team's overall case and summary of one's own case are important.

Refutation: The process of explaining why an opponent's arguments are incorrect. Involves point by point clash in the constructive speeches and overall refutation in the rebuttals. A debater may refute an opponent's points on a variety of grounds, such as irrelevant information, contradictory statements, or faulty logic.

Resolution: The topic of the debate, generally presented as a statement and preceded by a phrase such as "Be it resolved that" (BIRT) or "This House believes that" (THBT). Its terms need to be interpreted and clarified by the Affirmative team. The resolution is supported by the Affirmative team and opposed by the Negative team.

Script speaking: Delivery using a word for word text. This method is commonly used by beginners who aren't yet comfortable with having only an outline. It's also used by speakers who need to present precise thoughts and words, such as scientists and politicians.

Speaker: The moderator of a parliamentary debate. The Speaker introduces each debater and rules on Points of Order and Points of Personal Privilege. Debaters address their arguments through the Speaker, as is the case in functioning legislatures.

Specific knowledge: An impromptu debate situation in which the Affirmative team presents a case that relies on facts not commonly known, often of a scientific or historical nature. A specific knowledge case may place the Negative team at an unfair disadvantage.

Status quo: How the current system operates. The Affirmative team in a policy debate will propose changing the status quo, whereas the Negative team will usually defend the present system.

SWOT analysis: The process of looking closely at the Strengths, Weaknesses, Opportunities, and Threats of a debate case. This method can be used to evaluate and make improvements to a case before presenting it in a debate round.

THBT: An abbreviation for "This House believes that" placed before a resolution in parliamentary debate, generally of a values nature.

Theme: A general idea that's supported by several points. In a team's case, there are typically one or two central themes. Debaters commonly talk about their themes as a way of tying together and providing context to different arguments.

THW: An abbreviation for "This House would" placed before a parliamentary debate resolution, usually of a policy nature.

Time-place-set: A type of definition in which the Affirmative team lays out a situation for debate, either a fictional or real scenario or a point in history. Each team must debate within these parameters, without bringing in details that wouldn't be known at the time or place.

Transition: Moving from one point to another such that the speech flows smoothly. Usually tells the audience what has just been accomplished and what can be expected next.

Truism: A definition of a resolution that's always true, making it virtually impossible to debate. Truisms are not allowed, as they place the Negative team in an unfair position.

Values debate: A debate focusing on competing principles, rather than on a plan of action. The teams argue whether a particular circumstance or idea is right or wrong.

Bibliography

Many of the web resources that are listed below have been useful references for this publication. Since the space limitations of a single book made it impossible to cover fully the expansive field of speech and debate, they will provide useful supplementary information on tournaments, styles, and techniques.

You may also find within these resources perspectives that are different than what you've read in this book. These perspectives are neither right nor wrong, as speech and debate is a subjective art interpreted differently by a variety of people. In the true spirit of debate, you're encouraged to evaluate these resources for yourself and to determine what works best for you.

Alberta Debate and Speech Association
http://www.compusmart.ab.ca/adebate

Australian Debating Federation
http://www.adf.asn.au

Canadian Student Debating Federation
http://www.csdf-fcde.ca

Canadian University Society of Intercollegiate Debate
http://www.cusid.ca

Cross-Examination Debate Association
http://www.cedadebate.org

Debatabase
http://www.debatabase.com

Debate Central
http://debate.uvm.edu

English-Speaking Union
http://www.britishdebate.com

International Debate Education Association
http://www.idebate.org

***Debating* by Simon Quinn**
http://www.learndebating.com

Manitoba Speech and Debate Association
http://www.sjr.mb.ca/debate

National Forensics League
http://www.nflonline.org

National Parliamentary Debate Association
http://www.parlidebate.org

Ontario Student Debating Union
http://www.osdu.oise.utoronto.ca

On That Point
http://www.onthatpoint.com

Queensland Debating Union
http://www.qdu.org.au

World Schools Debating Championships
http://www.schoolsdebate.com

Acknowledgments

To say that this book is "by Alim Merali" alone would be giving myself too much credit. I didn't make any new discoveries, nor did I invent any novel methods. I am not a pioneer in the field, but a beneficiary of it. My contribution to this book was compiling information and insights taught to me by many people over many years. To these individuals, I offer my sincere gratitude.

First and foremost, I want to thank the leaders who made competitive speech and debate possible for me. In particular, many people within the Alberta Debate and Speech Association deserve my appreciation. Dozens of dedicated volunteers, particularly debate coaches and tournament directors, gave up weekend after weekend to allow me to take up my passion for debating. Hundreds of judges provided priceless advice and continual encouragement.

Over seven years as a competitive debater, I had the opportunity to work with dozens of partners in hundreds of tournament and practice rounds. I want to thank my debate partners from the Old Scona Academic High School Debate Society, the University of Alberta Debate Society, and the University of Western Ontario Debate Society. We relished our victories together, and we reflected on our defeats together. We helped each other build on what we did right and improve on what we did wrong. Since I believe that the greatest source of knowledge is experience (the topic of one of my tougher debate rounds), it's clear to me that my experiences in competitive debating have contributed immensely to this book.

My competitors provided the rivalry that made debate enjoyable and challenging. While they may have been more dedicated to defeating me than to helping me, they acted as indispensable 'sounding boards' for my arguments. The spirit of competition brought out the best in each of us, and I know that we shared some great moments (read: intense, nail-biting battles) over many years.

Some of my best debate experiences have come well outside the world of competitive debate. I want to thank the people who have challenged me as I've put my debate skills into practice. At the University of Western Ontario's Richard Ivey School of Business, my fellow students have pushed me to defend my views during literally hundreds of challenging debates on real business cases. My associates in the world of politics have encouraged me to articulate and defend my opinions on the issues that shape society. It is from the intelligent and well-spoken people I am privileged to be surrounded by every day that I have experienced the ultimate test in debate.

Finally, thank you to the friends and family who told me to "keep pushing it" when I stalled for a while, unsure of what to write next. Although authoring this book took longer than I had originally anticipated (and promised), I hope that you've found it worth the wait.

Index

About the Author

Alim Merali is a past Canadian Student Debating Federation National Champion. He developed the debate training program at The Speech Studio Inc., a speech communication academy. Alim has coached speech and debate at high schools and has directed the Alberta Debate Championships and the Alberta Model Legislature. He serves on the Alberta Debate and Speech Association's Board of Directors.

Looking for short, to the point debate resources?
Want a quick refresher on *Talk the Talk*?
If so, visit us on the web ...

talkthetalk.ca